25 beaded knits

25 beaded knits

Debbie Abrahams

COLLINS & BROWN

This book is dedicated to my wonderful parents, Tom and Heddy Abrahams.

First published in the United Kingdom in 2007 by
Collins & Brown
10 Southcombe Street
London
W14 0RA

An imprint of Anova Books Company Ltd

ISBN 978-1-84340-424-8

A CIP catalogue for this book is available from the British Library.

9 8 7 6 5 4 3 2 1

Reproduction by Rival Colour Ltd, UK
Printed and bound by SNP Leefung, China.

This book can be ordered direct from the publisher.
Contact the marketing department, but try your bookshop first.

www.anovabooks.com

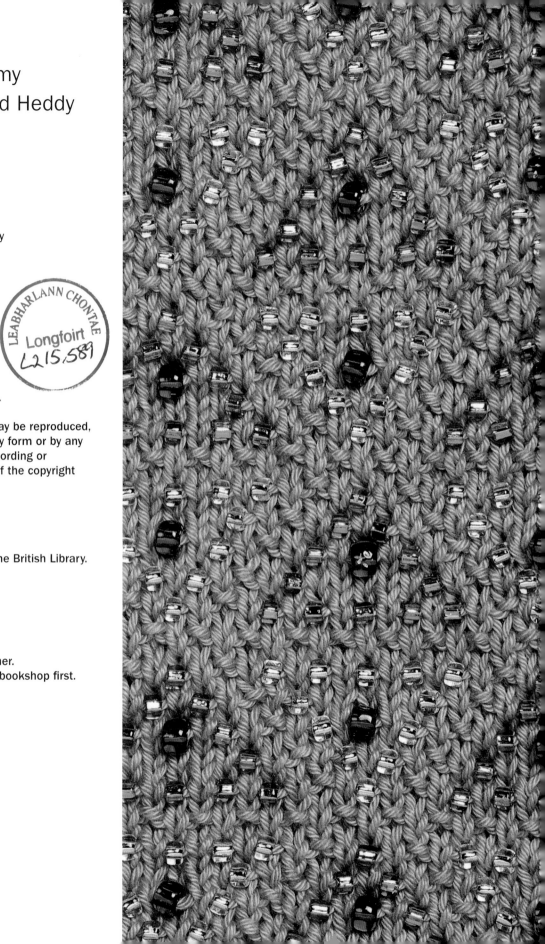

Contents

Introduction

Knitting with beads is fun and easy to do and it can be used to transform a very ordinary-looking fabric into something quite dazzling. I first came across the technique many years ago, when I first started to design my own patterns, and, became hooked very quickly – it's so addictive!

In this book I have designed a collection of projects that include home furnishings, fashion accessories and garments, which will keep both the novice knitter and the more experienced knitter busy. Each project is marked with a difficulty rating, so everyone can confidently knit something sparkly and special. Coloured beads on a single colour of yarn, result in subtle, sophisticated fabrics, while multicoloured bead designs, create exciting patterns. Experienced knitters might want to try the projects that combine colour knitting with beads, which take the whole technique a step further – a little more difficult, but certainly still very enjoyable.

I had lots of fun designing these projects, so I hope that you have just as much fun knitting them. But make sure that you are prepared for a life-changing moment – because once you have knitted with beads, you will never look back!

☆ Beginner

☆☆ Intermediate

☆☆☆ Advanced

These are a guide only. What some knitters find difficult, others find quite easy, so read the pattern before deciding whether or not to knit it.

Cosy at Home

Aladdin Slippers

These fun slippers combine beads and stripes with alternating colours to give them a slightly humorous and theatrical look. They are ideal for wearing around the house or in bed to keep your feet warm and cosy.

SIZE
One size

MATERIALS
Pair 5.00mm (US 8) needles
Pair 4.50mm (US 7) needles
One 4.50mm (US 7) circular
    needle, 40cm (16in) long

Yarn
Rowan *Pure Wool DK*
50g (1¾oz) per ball
    (A) 006 Pier   1
    (B) 040 Tangerine   1
    (C) 017 Mocha   1
Use yarn double throughout

Extras
Beads: 80 × 5mm (³⁄₁₆in) turquoise
    beads
More yarn might be required if the
slippers are knitted to a longer
length

TENSION (GAUGE)
17 sts and 25 rows to 10cm (4in)
measured over stocking
(stockinette) stitch using 5.00mm
(US 8) needles and yarn double.

NOTE
Both slippers are knitted to the
same shape, but the colours are
different.

KNIT
Slipper 1
Begin at heel and work toward the
toe. Thread 40 beads on yarn A.
Using yarn A and 5.00mm (US 8)
needles, cast on 26 sts.
NEXT ROW (RS) (INCREASE): K11,
inc once knitwise into next st, k1,
inc once knitwise into next st, K to
end. (28 sts)
NEXT ROW (WS): Purl.
NEXT ROW (RS) (INCREASE): K11,
inc 1 knitwise into next st, k3, inc
1 knitwise into next st, K to end.
(30 sts)
NEXT ROW (WS): Purl.
NEXT ROW (RS) (INCREASE): K11,
inc 1 knitwise into next st, k5, inc
1 knitwise into next st, K to end.
(32 sts)
NEXT ROW (WS): Purl.
NEXT ROW (RS)
(INCREASE): K11,
inc 1 knitwise into next
st, k7, inc 1 knitwise
into next st, K to end.
(34 sts)
NEXT ROW (WS): Purl.
NEXT ROW (RS)
(INCREASE): K11, inc 1
knitwise into next st,
k9, inc 1 knitwise into
next st, K to end.
(36 sts)
NEXT ROW (WS): Purl.

BEADED PATT REP:
ROW 1 (RS): Using yarn
A, knit.

ROW 2 (WS): K12, p12, k12.
ROW 3 (RS): Knit.
ROW 4 (WS): Purl.
ROW 5 (RS): K2, (pb, k1) 5 times,
k13, (pb, k1) 5 times, k1.
ROW 6 (WS): As Row 2.
ROW 7 (RS): Using yarn B, knit.
ROW 8 (WS): Using yarn B, purl.
ROWS 9–10: Rep Rows 7–8.
Rep the 10-row patt rep until the
slipper, when slightly stretched, is
approximately 5cm (2in) shorter
than the length from heel to toe,
ending after either Row 6 or Row
10.

Change to 4.50mm (US 7) needles
and yarn C.
NEXT ROW (RS): Knit.

NEXT ROW (WS) (INCREASE): (K1,
p1) 9 times, M1, (p1, k1) 9 times.
(37 sts)
NEXT ROW (RS): (K1, p1) to last st,
k1.
NEXT ROW (WS): (K1, p1) to last st,
k1.
Rep the last 2 rows until slipper,
when slightly stretched, fits from
heel to toe.
NEXT ROW (RS) (DECREASE): [K1,
k2tog, (p1, k1) 3 times, p1, k2tog
3 times, k1. (31 sts)
NEXT ROW (WS): Purl.
NEXT ROW (RS) (DECREASE): (K1,
k2tog, k5, k2tog) 3 times, k1.
(25 sts)
NEXT ROW (WS): Purl.

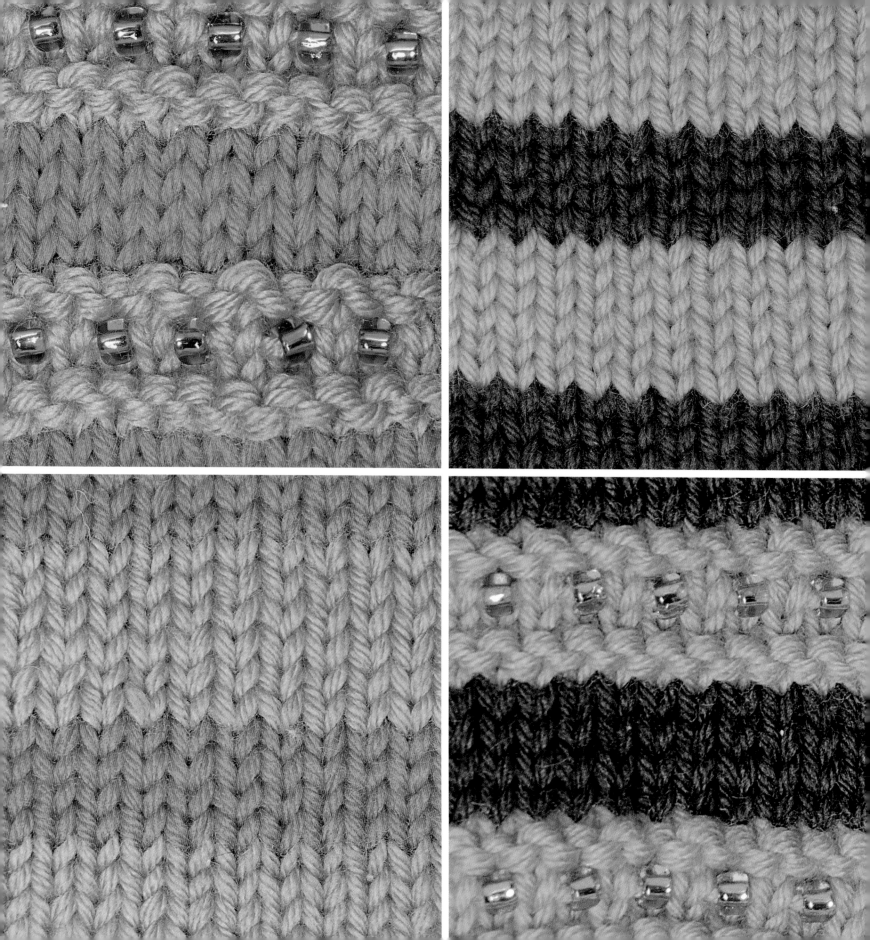

NEXT ROW (RS) (DECREASE): (K1, k2tog, k3, k2tog) 3 times, k1. (19 sts)
Break yarn leaving a 15cm (6in) tail.
Using a needle, draw up yarn tightly through sts.

Slipper 2

Rep instructions for slipper 1, but change colours throughout as foll:
Use yarn B in place of C.
Use yarn C in place of B.
Yarn A remains the same.

FINISHING

Sew in any loose ends on the WS of the work. Join heel.
    Using photograph as a guide, join top of slipper from end of toe to beg of moss (seed) stitch.

Edging (slipper 1)

With RS facing, using yarn B and 4.50mm (US 7) circular needle and beg at the top of the heel, pick up and knit 70 sts around top edge of slipper (or as many sts are required for the sts to sit evenly – you are now knitting on the round). Mark the first st of the round.
NEXT ROUND: Purl.
NEXT ROUND: Purl.
With RS facing, cast (bind) off sts purlwise.
Sew in any loose ends on the WS of the work.

Edging (slipper 2)

Rep instructions for edging for slipper 1, but use yarn C in place of yarn B.

Foot loose and fancy free

If preferred an aran weight yarn could be used instead of two strands of double-knitting. Just check the tension of the aran yarn on the ball-band, if the tension matches, you can use it.

Bubbly Knitting Bag

Bright bubblegum pink and soft ice-blue are combined in this cute bag, which can be used to store away all your knitting accessories. The bag is long enough to accommodate most knitting needles, and the handy pockets on both front and back panels can be used for smaller bits and pieces such as yarn bobbins, sewing needles and stitch markers.

SIZE
34cm × 16.5cm (13in × 6½in)

MATERIALS
Pair 3.00mm (US 2–3) needles
Pair 3.75mm (US 5) needles
One 3.75mm (US 5) circular
   needle, 40cm (16in) long

Yarn
Rowan *Handknit Cotton*
50g (1¾oz) per ball

(A) 313 Slick		2
(B) 327 Aqua		2
(C) 310 Shell		2
(D) 332 Rose		1

Extras
Beads: 162 × 5mm (³⁄₁₆in)
   turquoise beads
2 Pink plastic buttons
Pink ribbon: 50cm (20in)

TENSION (GAUGE)
22 sts and 30 rows to 10cm (4in)
measured over stocking
(stockinette) stitch using 3.75mm
(US 5) needles.

KNIT
Base Panel
Using yarn A and 3.00mm (US 2–3) needles, cast on 75 sts.
ROW 1 (RS): K1, (p1, k1) to end of row.
ROW 2 (WS): K1, (p1, k1) to end of row.
Rep the last 2 rows 13 times more, ending with a WS row.
Cast (bind) off sts knitwise.

Pocket lining 1 (for front panel)
Do not break off yarns at the end of rows. Carry them up the side of the work.
Using yarn C and 3.75mm (US 5) circular needle, cast on 25 sts.
Beg with a RS row, work in stripe patt rep as folls:
*ROW 1 (RS): Using yarn C, knit.
ROW 2 (WS): Using yarn C, purl.
ROW 3 (RS): Using yarn C, knit.
ROW 4 (WS): Using yarn D, purl.
ROW 5 (RS): Using yarn D, knit.
ROW 6 (WS): Using yarn D, purl.
Push the sts to the other end of the circular needle so that the WS of the work is facing you again.
ROW 7 (WS): Using yarn C, purl.
ROW 8 (RS): Using yarn C, knit.
ROW 9 (WS): Using yarn C, purl.
ROW 10 (RS): Using yarn D, knit.
ROW 11 (WS): Using yarn D, purl.
ROW 12 (RS): Using yarn D, knit.
Push the sts to the other end of the circular needle so that the RS of the work is facing you again.*
Rep from * to * twice more, but after the last row do not push the sts to the other end of the needle.
Break off both yarns and leave sts on a holder.

Pocket lining 2 (for back panel)
Rep instructions for pocket lining 1 but use yarn B in place of yarn C.

Front panel
Note: Yarn B will need to be divided into separate balls to knit the panel. Thread several beads onto each ball of yarn B.
With RS facing and using 3.00mm (US 2–3) needles, pick up and knit 75 sts along cast-on edge of base panel as foll:
15B, 11A, 18B, 11C, 12B, 5D, 3B.

Change to 3.75mm (US 5) needles.
NEXT ROW (WS) (INCREASE): Inc 1 purlwise into first st using yarn B, p1B, p7D, p10B, p13C, p17B, p11A, p13B, inc once purlwise into next st using yarn B, p1. (77 sts)

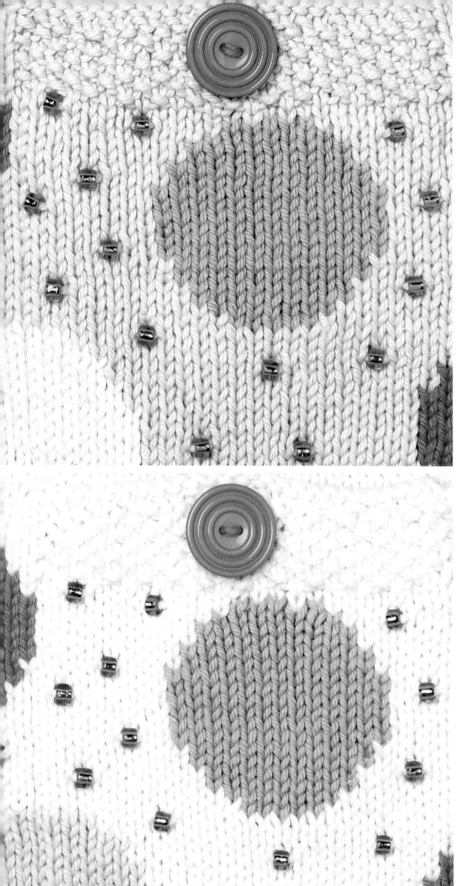

Beg with a RS row, work chart rows 1–32, ending with a WS row.

Pocket top

Cont to work chart rows 33–36, working the centre 25 sts in moss (seed) stitch as indicated on the chart for pocket top.

CHART ROW 37 (RS) (BUTTONHOLE): K13B, k5C, k8B, (p1B, k1B) 5 times, p1B, cast (bind) off next 3 sts, (p1B, k1B) 5 times which includes the st already on RH needle, p1B, k22B, k4C.

CHART ROW 38 (WS): P3C, p4B, pb, p19B, (k1B, p1B) 5 times, turn work, cast on 3 sts, turn work again, (p1B, k1B) 5 times, p27B. Cont to work chart rows 39–40, ending with a WS row.

JOIN POCKET LINING:
Use yarn B only.

NEXT ROW (RS): K3, pb, k22, bind (cast) off next 25 sts purlwise, sl the st on the RH needle onto the LH needle, then with RS facing, sl the sts for the pocket lining onto the RH needle, sl the first st on the LH needle back onto the RH needle then knit across the rem sts on the LH needle.

NEXT ROW (WS): P4, pb, p12, pb, p8, purl across 25 sts of pocket lining, p8, pb, p17. Work 2 rows in stocking (stockinette) stitch (knit on RS rows; purl on WS rows).

Top Edging

Use 3.00mm (US 2–3) needles. Thread 37 beads on yarn C. Knit 2 rows using yarn A. Knit 2 rows using yarn D. Knit 3 rows using yarn C. Purl 1 row using yarn C.

NEXT ROW (RS): Using yarn C, k2, (pb, k1) 36 times, pb, k2.

NEXT ROW (WS): Using yarn C, knit.

Knit 2 rows using yarn D. Knit 1 row using yarn A. With WS facing and using yarn A, cast (bind) off sts knitwise.

Back panel

Rep instructions for front panel but change colours throughout as foll:
    Use B in place of C.
    Use C in place of B.
    All other colours remain the same.

Side gusset 1

*With RS facing and using yarn A and 3.00mm (US 2–3) needles, pick up and knit 14 sts along one short end of base panel.

NEXT ROW (WS) (INCREASE): Inc 1 knitwise into first st, p5, k2, p5, inc once knitwise into last st. (16 sts) Change to 3.75mm (US 5) needles.

NEXT ROW (RS) (INCREASE): P2, (k1, inc 1 knitwise into each of next 3 sts, k1, p2) twice. (22 sts)

NEXT ROW (WS): K2, (p8, k2) twice.

CABLE PATT REP:
ROW 1 (RS): P2, (k8, p2) twice.
ROW 2 (WS): K2, (p8, k2) twice.
ROWS 3–4: Rep Rows 1–2.
ROW 5 (RS): P2, (c8f, p2) twice.
ROW 6 (WS): As Row 2.
ROWS 7–16: Rep Rows 1–2, 5 times.
ROWS 17–40: Rep Rows 5–16 twice. Change to 3.00mm (US 2–3) needles.
ROWS 41–51: Rep Rows 5–15 once.
ROW 52 (WS) (DECREASE): K2tog, (p2tog) 4 times, k2tog, (p2tog) 4 times, k2tog. (11 sts)
Put a marker at the beg and end of Row 52.
ROW 53 (RS): P1, sl next 5 sts on cable needle and hold at front of work, k4 from LH needle, sl 1 st

CHART

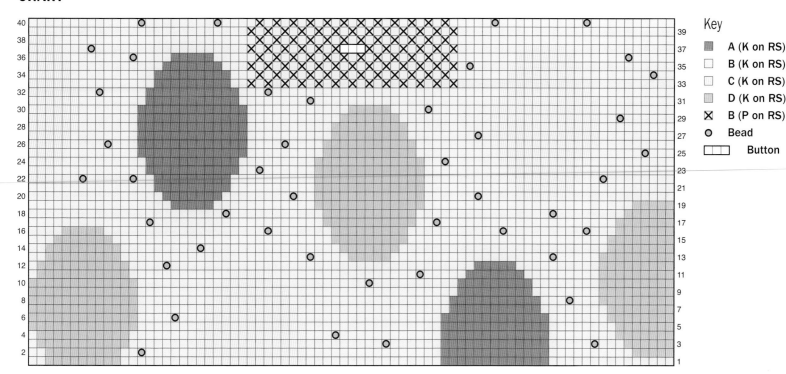

Key

- ▨ A (K on RS)
- ☐ B (K on RS)
- ☐ C (K on RS)
- ▨ D (K on RS)
- ☒ B (P on RS)
- ○ Bead
- ☐☐☐ Button

back onto LH needle and purl it, k4 from cable needle, p1.
ROW 54 (WS): K1, (P4, K1) twice.

Strap (using yarn A only)

CABLE PATT REP:

ROW 1 (RS): P1, (k4, p1) twice.
ROW 2 (WS): K1, (p4, k1) twice.
ROWS 3–8: Rep Rows 1–2, 3 times.
ROW 9 (RS): P1, sl next 5 sts on cable needle and hold at front of work, k4 sts from LH needle, sl 1 st back onto LH needle and knit it, k4 sts from cable needle, p1.
ROW 10 (WS): K1, (p4, k1) twice.
ROWS 11–12: Rep Rows 1–2.
Rep Rows 1–12 until strap is half required length, ending after Row 12 of the cable pattern.*
Break yarn and leave sts on a holder.

Side gusset 2

Rep instructions for side gusset 1 and strap from * to *.
With RS facing (and making sure that the strap is not twisted), join both ends of the strap by casting (binding) off both sets of sts together.

FINISHING

Lining is optional. But if you want to line the bag it is advisable to cut the lining fabric before sewing the bag together: lay bag on lining fabric and cut out one piece the same size as sides, gusset and base shape, adding seam allowances where gussets will meet sides. Sew the side seams of the lining together. Put to one side.

Sew in any loose ends on the WS of the work.

With WS facing and using a pressing cloth, lightly press the panels.

Sew pocket linings into place.

Join side gussets to side edges of back and front panels, matching Row 52 (decrease row) of the side gussets to the top edge of the bag.

Sew buttons to pocket linings on back and front panels, to correspond with buttonholes.

Cut the ribbon into two equal pieces. Sew one to the inside of the bag at top edge of front panel, ensuring that it is in the centre.

Rep for back panel.

Slip the lining into the bag. Turn in the hem along the top edge and stitch to the bag.

Organic Cushion Cover

The broad horizontal stripes in alternating shades of lime, olive and gold are punctuated with red beads and autumnal bobbles, warming the colour palette and adding textural interest to the finished piece. The back of the cushion is fastened very simply with five ceramic buttons in an earthy shade of brown. The cushion complements the Organic Blanket on page 26.

SIZE
38cm × 38cm (15in × 15in).

MATERIALS
Pair 3.75mm (US 5) needles
Pair 3.00mm (US 2–3) needles
Cable needle

Yarn
Rowan *Classic Cashsoft DK*
50g (1¾oz) balls
(A) 523 Lichen		2
(B) 510 Clementine		
	small amount	
(C) 521 Opulence		
	small amount	
(D) 509 Lime		2
(E) 522 Cashew		2

Extras
Beads: 44 × 5mm (³⁄₁₆in)
red beads
5 Brown ceramic buttons

TENSION (GAUGE)
24 sts and 32 rows to 10cm (4in) measured over stocking (stockinette) stitch using 3.75mm (US 5) needles

SPECIAL ABBREVIATIONS
c8b = slip next 5 sts onto cable needle and hold at front of work, k3 from LH needle, then k5 from cable needle
c8f = slip next 3 sts onto cable needle and hold at front of work, k5 from LH needle, the k3 from cable needle
mb = using contrast yarn (joined into work on the row before) k into front, back, front, back, front of next st, turn work (WS facing), p5, turn work again (RS facing), k5, slip 2–5th sts over 1st st, pull firmly on yarn to tighten bobble and knot ends to secure later.

KNIT
Front panel
Thread beads onto yarns as foll:
    yarn A: 8 beads
    yarn D: 24 beads
    yarn E: 12 beads
Using 3.00mm (US 2–3) needles and yarn A, cast (bind) on 93 sts.
NEXT ROW (RS) (INCREASE): Using yarn A, p2, [(inc once knitwise into next st, k1) twice, inc once knitwise into next st, p2, k3, p2] 7 times (inc once knitwise into next st, k1) twice, inc once knitwise into next st, p2. (117 sts)
NEXT ROW (WS): Using yarn A, k2, (p8, k2, p3, k2) 7 times, p8, k2.

Beg with a RS row, work chart rows 1–86, rep the 30 st patt rep 3 times across each row as indicated on the chart.
Rep chart rows 15–50, ending with a WS row.

NEXT ROW (RS): P2E, (k4E, pb, k3E, p2E, c3fE, p2E, k3E, MbB, k4E, p2E, c3fE, p2E) 3 times, k4E, pb, k3E, p2E, c3fE, p2E, k3E, MbB, k4E, p2E.
NEXT ROW (WS): Using yarn E, k2, (p8, k2, p3, k2) 7 times, p8, k2.
NEXT ROW (RS) (DECREASE): Using yarn E, p2, [(k2tog, k1) twice, k2tog, p2, k3, p2] 7 times, (k2tog, k1) twice, k2tog, p2. (93 sts)
With WS facing and using yarn E, cast (bind) off sts purlwise.

Upper back panel
With RS facing and using yarn C and 3.00mm (US 2–3) needles, pick up and knit 93 sts along the cast-off edge of front panel.
NEXT ROW (WS): Using yarn C, knit.
Change to 3.75mm (US 5) needles.
*Working in stocking (stockinette) stitch (knit on RS rows, purl on WS rows) and beg with a RS row, cont to work in stripe patt rep as foll:
    yarn A: 4 rows
    yarn D: 2 rows
    yarn E: 4 rows

    yarn D: 2 rows
Rep the 12 row patt rep 4 times more, ending with a WS row.
Change to 3.00mm (US 2–3) needles and yarn A.
NEXT ROW (RS): Using yarn A, knit.
NEXT ROW (WS): Using yarn A, k1, (p1, k1) to end of row.
NEXT ROW (RS): Using yarn A, k1, (p1, k1) to end of row.
Rep the last 2 rows once more.*
NEXT ROW (WS) (BUTTONHOLE): Using yarn A, k1, (p1, k1) twice, [cast (bind) off next 3 sts, (k1, p1) 8 times which includes the st already on RH needle, k1] 4 times, cast (bind) off next 3 sts, (k1, p1) twice, k1.
NEXT ROW (RS): Using yarn A, k1, (p1, k1) twice, [turn work, cast on 3 sts, turn work again, (k1, p1) 8 times, k1] 4 times, turn work, cast on 3 sts, turn work again, (k1, p1) twice, k1.
NEXT ROW (WS): Using yarn A, k1, (p1, k1) to end of row.
NEXT ROW (RS): using yarn A, k1, (p1, k1) to end of row.
NEXT ROW (WS): Using yarn A, k1, (p1, k1) to end of row.
With RS facing and using yarn A, cast (bind) off sts knitwise.

Lower back panel
With RS facing and using yarn C and 3.00mm (US 2–3) needles,

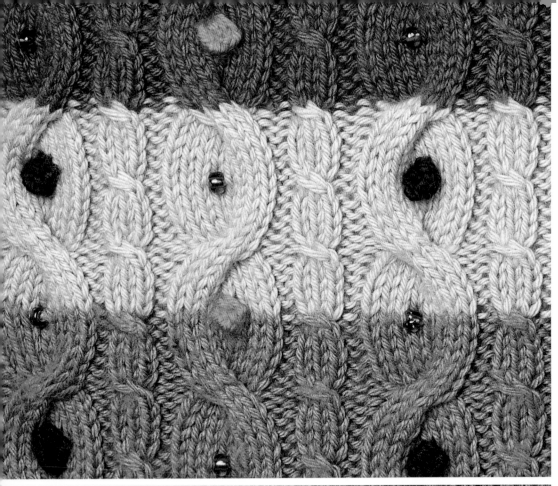

pick up and knit 93 sts along the cast-on edge of front panel.

NEXT ROW (WS): Using yarn C, knit. Change to 3.75mm (US 5) needles.

Rep instructions for upper back panel from * to *.

NEXT ROW (WS): K1, (p1, k1) to end of row.

NEXT ROW (RS): K1, (p1, k1) to end of row.

Rep the last 2 rows 7 times more. With WS facing and using yarn A, cast (bind) off sts purlwise.

CHART

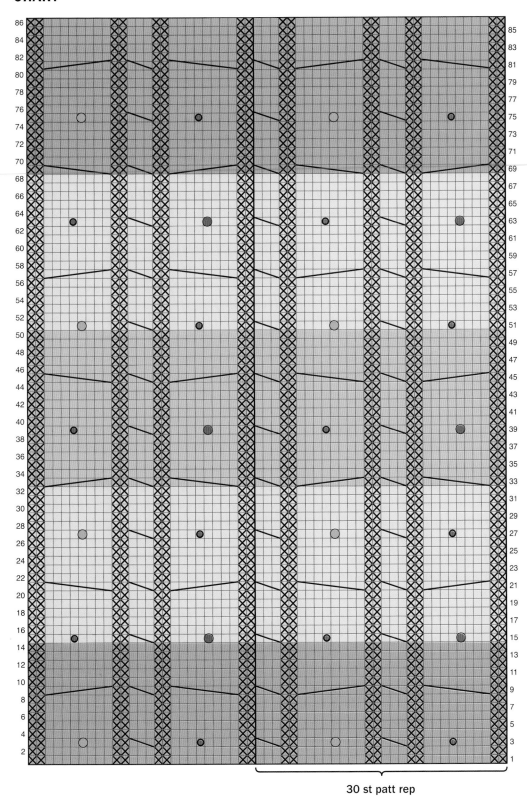

30 st patt rep

Key

- ▦ A (K on RS)
- ▢ D (K on RS)
- ▦ E (K on RS)
- ⊠ A (P on RS)
- ⊠ D (P on RS)
- ⊠ E (P on RS)
- ● C (make bobble)
- ● B (make bobble)
- ● Bead

—— C8F
—— C8B
—— C3F

FINISHING

Sew in any loose ends on the WS of the work. With WS facing and using a pressing cloth, lightly press the cushion cover. Mark the center point along side seam edges of front panel.

Join side seams of upper back panel to front panel, ensuring that the buttonholes on back panel match the marked center point on front panel. Join side seams of lower back panel to front panel, inserting the seed (moss) st border at finished edge under the finished edge of the upper back panel, and sew down into place.

Turn cover inside-out and press seams.

Sew buttons onto lower back panel to correspond with buttonholes.

Slouch Socks

These comfy socks, knitted in a luxuriously soft cashmere yarn, will make you feel really special. What better way to spend a lazy evening than curled up on the sofa with your feet kept warm and sparkling in these gorgeous socks!

SIZE

One size (foot can be knitted to desired length)

MATERIALS

4.00mm (US 6) needle
Set 3.00mm (US 2–3) four dp needles
Set 3.75mm (US 5) four dp needles

Yarn

Rowan *Classic Cashsoft DK*
50g (1¾oz) per ball
  (A) 503 Mirage   2
  (B) 502 Bella Donna 2
  More yarn might be required
  if the foot is knitted to a
  longer length.

Extras

Beads: 800 × 3mm (⅛in)
  blue beads

TENSION (GAUGE)

28 sts and 36 rows to 10cm (4in) measured over stocking (stockinette) stitch using 3.00mm (US 2–3) needles

KNIT

Make two socks the same.

Ribbing

Thread 400 beads on yarn B.
Using yarn A, cast on 49 sts onto one 4.00mm (US 6) needle.
Divide the sts as foll between three 3.00mm (US 2–3) dp needles:
  16 sts on first needle
  16 sts on second needle
  17 sts on third needle.
NEXT ROW (RS) (JOIN THE ROUND): Using yarn A, sl the last cast-on st on third needle onto the LH needle and knit it together with the first st on the first needle, then (p1, k1) 23 times, p1. (48 sts)
Mark the first st of the round.
ROUND 1: Using yarn A, k1, (p1, k1) 23 times, p1.
ROUNDS 2–4: Work 3 rounds as last round.
ROUND 5: Using yarn B, k1, (p1, k1) 23 times, p1.
ROUNDS 6–7: Work 2 rounds as last round.
ROUNDS 8–11: Rep Rounds 1–4.
ROUNDS 12: As Round 1.
NEXT ROUND (INCREASE): Using yarn B, k1, (inc once knitwise into each of next 2 sts, k1) 15 times, inc once knitwise into each of next 2 sts. (80 sts)
Change to 3.75mm (US 5) dp needles.
NEXT ROUND: Using yarn B, knit.

Leg

Using yarn B only, work beaded patt as folls:
ROUND 1: K8, (pb, k9) 7 times, pb, k1.
ROUND 2: K6, (pb, k9) 7 times, pb, k3.
ROUND 3: K4, (pb, k9) 7 times, pb, k5.
ROUND 4: K2, (pb, k9) 7 times, pb, k7.
ROUND 5: Knit.
ROUND 6: K1, (pb, k9) 7 times, pb, k8.
ROUND 7: Knit.
ROUND 8: K2, (pb, k9) 7 times, pb, k7.
ROUND 9: K4, (pb, k9) 7 times, pb, k5.
ROUND 10: K6, (pb, k9) 7 times, pb, k3.
ROUND 11: K8, (pb, k9) 7 times, pb, k1.
ROUND 12: Knit.
ROUND 13: K9, (pb, k9) 7 times, pb.
ROUND 14: Knit.
Rep rounds 1–14, 4 times more.

Change to 3.00mm (US 2–3) dp needles.
NEXT ROUND (DECREASE): Using yarn B, k1, [(k2tog) twice, k1] 15 times, (k2tog) twice. (48 sts)
Using yarn B, knit 2 rounds.

Heel flap

Slip the last 12 sts of the last round onto a free needle, then using yarn B, knit the first 12 sts of the last round onto the same needle. (24 sts)
Slip the rem 24 sts onto a holder to be worked later for the instep. Turn work.
NOTE: You are now working back and forth across rows and not in the round.
ROW 1 (WS): Using yarn A, sl 1 purlwise, purl across row.
ROW 2 (RS): Using yarn A, sl 1 knitwise, knit across row.
Rep Rows 1–2 until heel flap measures 7cm (2.75in), ending by working a RS row.
TURNING THE HEEL
ROW 1 (WS): Using yarn A, p14, p2tog, p1.
Turn, leaving rem 7 sts unworked.
ROW 2 (RS): Using yarn A, sl 1 knitwise, k5, ssk, k1.
Turn, leaving rem 7 sts unworked.
ROW 3 (WS): Using yarn A, sl 1 purlwise, p6, p2tog, p1.
Turn, leaving rem 5 sts unworked.
ROW 4 (RS): Using yarn A, sl 1 knitwise, k7, ssk, k1.
Turn, leaving rem 5 sts unworked.
ROW 5 (WS): Using yarn A, sl 1 purlwise, p8, p2tog, p1.
Turn, leaving rem 3 sts unworked.
ROW 6 (RS): Using yarn A, sl 1 knitwise, k9, ssk, k1.
Turn, leaving rem 3 sts unworked.

ROW 7 (WS): Using yarn A, sl 1 purlwise, p10, p2tog, p1.
Turn, leaving rem st unworked.
ROW 8 (RS): Using yarn A, sl 1 knitwise, k11, ssk, k1.
Turn, leaving rem st unworked.
ROW 9 (WS): Using yarn A, sl 1 purlwise, p12, p2tog, turn.
ROW 10 (RS): Using yarn A, sl 1 knitwise, k12, ssk.
This leaves 14 sts.

Gusset

With RS of heel flap facing toward you and using yarn A and a free needle, pick up and knit 13 sts along left side of heel flap; on second free needle knit across 24 sts from stitch holder for instep; on third free needle pick up and knit 13 sts along right side of heel flap, then knit 7 sts of heel flap onto same needle.
Slip rem 7 sts of heel flap onto beg of first needle. (64 sts)

NOTE: You are now knitting in the round again.
ROUND 1: Using yarn A, on first needle knit to last 3 sts, k2tog, k1, on second needle k24, and on third needle k1, ssk, knit rem sts.
ROUND 2: Using yarn A, knit.
Rep the the last 2 rounds 7 times more. (48 sts)

Foot

Using yarn A, work with needles in rounds until foot measures approximately 5cm (2in) shorter than the desired length of the sock.
NEXT ROUND: Using yarn B, knit.

Toe shaping

ROUND 1: Using yarn B, on first needle knit to last 3 sts, k2tog, k1, on second needle k1, ssk, K to last 3 sts, k2tog, k1, and on third needle k1, ssk, K rem sts.
ROUND 2: Using yarn B, knit.
ROUNDS 3–12: Rep Rounds 1–2, 5 times. (24 sts)

ROUNDS 13–14: Rep Round 1 twice. (16 sts)
Knit sts from first needle onto second needle.
There are now 8 sts on each of the two needles.
Break yarn, leaving a long tail for joining the toe seam.
Join together the remaining sts at the toe using Kitchener stitch.
Sew in all ends.

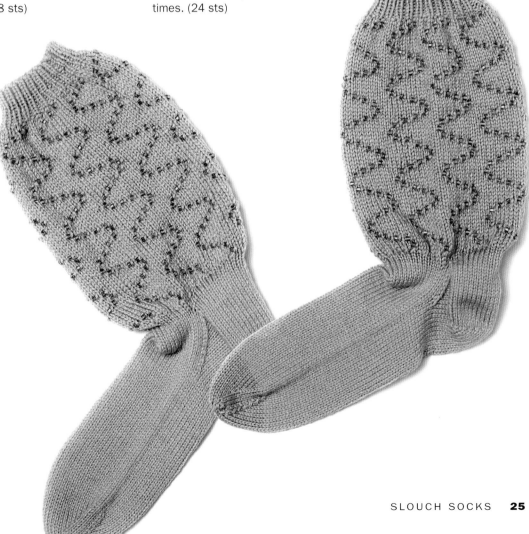

Organic Blanket

Inspired by patterns, shapes and colours found in vegetables and plants, this blanket combines cables, textured stitches, stripes, bobbles and beads to create a wonderful piece. The luxurious result would look great draped over a sofa or even you!

SIZE
119cm × 119cm (47in × 47in).

MATERIALS
Pair 3.75mm (US 5) needles
Two 3.25mm (US 3) circular
    needle, 100cm (39in) long
Cable needle

Yarn
Rowan *Classic Cashsoft DK*
50g (1¾oz) per ball
    (A) 510 Clementine   5
    (B) 523 Lichen   4
    (C) 509 Lime   4
    (D) 522 Cashew   4
    (E) 512 Poppy   4
    (F) 521 Opulence   4

Extras
Beads: 64 × 5mm (³⁄₁₆in) gold
    beads; same quantity in purple

TENSION (GAUGE)
24 sts and 32 rows to 10cm (4in)
measured over stocking
(stockinette) stitch using 3.75mm
(US 5) needles

SPECIAL ABBREVIATIONS
c7b = slip next 2 sts onto cable
needle and hold at front of work,
k1 from LH needle, slip 1 st back
onto LH needle and knit it, then K1
from cable needle

mb = using contrast yarn (joined
into work on the row before) k into
front, back, front, back, front of
next st, turn work (WS facing), p5,
turn work again (RS facing), k5, slip
2–5th sts over 1st st, pull firmly on
yarn to tighten bobble and knot
ends to secure later.

QUANTITY OF SQUARES
Peas and beans
    First colourway   4
    Second colourway   4
Basic stripe
    First colourway   6
    Second colourway   6
Organic cable
    First colourway   4
    Second colourway   4
Vegetable stripe
    First colourway   6
    Second colourway   6
Swirl
    First colourway   4
    Second colourway   5

KNIT
1a Peas and beans – first colourway
Using yarn A and 3.75mm (US 5)
needles, cast on 41 sts.
ROW 1 (RS) (INCREASE): Using yarn
A, p2, (inc once knitwise into each
of next 3 sts, k1, p2, k3, p2) 3
times, inc once knitwise into each
of next 3 sts, k1, p2. (53 sts)

ROW 2 (WS): Using yarn A, k2, (p7,
k2, p3, k2) 3 times, p7, k2.
ROW 3 (RS): Using yarn A, p2, (k7,
p2, c3f, p2) 3 times, k7, p2.
ROW 4 (WS): As Row 2.
ROW 5 (RS): Using yarn A, p2, (k7,
p2, k3, p2) 3 times, k7, p2.
ROW 6 (WS): K2A, (p3A, p1B, p3A,
k2A, p3A, k2A) 3 times, p3A, p1B,
p3A, k2A.
ROW 7 (RS): P2A, (k3A, MbB, k3A,
p2A, k3A, p2A) 3 times, k3A, MbB,
k3A, p2A.
ROWS 8–9: Rep Rows 2–3.
ROW 10 (WS): As Row 2.
ROW 11 (RS): As Row 5.
ROW 12 (WS): As Row 2.
ROW 13 (RS): Using yarn A, p2,
(c7b, p2, k3, p2) 3 times, c7b, p2.
ROW 14: As Row 2.
ROWS 15–26: As Rows 3–14 using
yarn C in place of B.
ROWS 27–38: As Rows 3–14 using
yarn D in place of C.
ROWS 39–50: As Rows 3–14.
ROWS 51–57: As Rows 15–21.

1b Peas and beans – second colourway
Follow instructions for first
colourway changing colours as folls:
    use D in place of A
    use F in place of B
    use A in place of C
    use E in place of D.

2a Basic stripe – first colourway
Using yarn C and 3.75mm (US 5)
needles, cast on 41 sts.
Working in plain stocking
(stockinette) stitch (knit on RS
rows, purl on WS rows), and beg
with a RS row, cont to work in
stripe patt rep as folls:
    yarn C: 2 rows
    yarn B: 4 rows
    yarn C: 2 rows
    yarn D: 4 rows.
Rep these 12 rows 3 times more.
    yarn C: 2 rows
    yarn B: 4 rows
    yarn C: 2 rows. (56 rows)
With RS facing and using yarn C,
cast (bind) off sts knitwise.

2b Basic stripe – second colourway
Follow instructions for first
colourway changing colours as folls:
    use A in place of C
    use F in place of B
    use E in place of D.

3a Organic cable – first colourway
Thread 16 gold beads on yarn E.
Using yarn E and 3.75mm (US 5)
needles, cast on 41 sts.
ROW 1 (RS) (INCREASE): P2, [(inc
once knitwise into next st, k1)
twice, inc once knitwise into next
st, p3] 4 times, (inc once knitwise
into next st, k1) twice, inc once
knitwise into next st, p2. (56 sts)

CHART

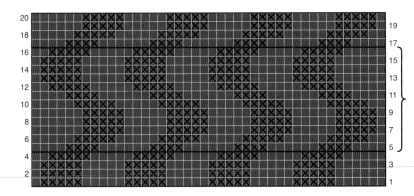

Key

▪	F (K on RS)
☒	F (P on RS)

12 row patt rep

ROW 2 (WS): K2, (p8, k3) 4 times, p8, k2.

CABLE PATT REP:
ROW 3 (RS): P2, (k8, p3) 4 times, k8, p2.
ROW 4 (WS): K2, (p8, k3) 4 times, p8, k2.
ROWS 5–6: Rep Rows 3–4.
ROW 7 (RS): P2, *sl next 3 sts onto cable needle and hold at front of work, k5 from LH needle, then k3 from cable needle, p3, sl next 5 sts onto cable needle and hold at back of work, k3 from LH needle, then K5 from cable needle*, p3, c8b, p3, rep from * to *, p2.
ROW 8 (WS): As Row 4.
ROWS 9–12: Rep Rows 3–4 twice.
ROW 13 (RS): P2, *k3, pb, k4, p3, k4, pb, k3*, p3, k8, p3, rep from * to *, p2.
ROW 14 (WS): As Row 4.
ROWS 15–18: Rep Rows 3–4 twice.
ROW 19 (RS): P2, * sl next 5 sts onto cable needle and hold at back of work, k3 from LH needle, then k5 from cable needle, p3, sl next 3 sts onto cable needle and hold at front of work, k5 from LH needle, then k3 from cable needle*, p3, c8b, p3, rep from * to *, p2.
ROW 20 (WS): As Row 4.
ROWS 21- 24: Rep Rows 3–4 twice.
ROW 25 (RS): P2, *k4, pb, k3, p3, k3, pb, k4*, p3, k8, p3, rep from * to *, p2.
ROW 26 (WS): As Row 4.

ROWS 27–30: Rep Rows 3–4 twice.
ROWS 31–54: Rep Rows 7–30.
ROW 55 (RS): As Row 7.
ROW 56 (WS): As Row 4.
ROW 57 (RS): As Row 3.
ROW 58 (WS) (DECREASE): K2, [(p2tog, p1) twice, p2tog, k3] 4 times, (p2tog, p1) twice, p2tog, k2. (41 sts)
With RS facing, cast (bind) off sts knitwise.

3b Organic cable – second colourway
Thread 16 purple beads onto yarn C.
Using yarn C and 3.75mm (US 5) needles, cast on 41 sts.
Follow instructions for first colourway using yarn C throughout.

4a Vegetable stripe – first colourway
Using yarn F and using 3.75mm (US 5) needles, cast on 41 sts.
Working in stocking (stockinette) stitch (knit on RS rows; purl on WS rows), and beg with a RS row cont in stripe patt as foll:
  yarn F: 6 rows
  yarn B: 5 rows
  yarn C: 2 rows
  yarn A: 6 rows
  yarn D: 6 rows
  yarn B: 2 rows
  yarn C: 5 rows
  yarn F: 4 rows
  yarn E: 3 rows

  yarn A: 6 rows
  yarn B: 4 rows
  yarn C: 3 rows
  yarn D : 4 rows. (56 rows)
With RS facing and using yarn D, cast (bind) off sts knitwise.

4b Vegetable stripe – second colourway
Follow instructions for first colourway but change colours as folls:
  use B in place of F
  use F in place of B
  use E in place of C
  use D in place of A
  use A in place of D
  use C in place of E.

5a Swirl – first colourway
Using yarn F and 3.75mm (US 5) needles, cast on 42 sts.
Beg with a RS row, work chart Rows 1–16.
Rep chart Rows 5–16, 3 times.
Work chart Rows 17–20. (56 rows)
With RS facing, cast (bind) off sts knitwise.

5b Swirl – second colourway
Follow instructions for first colourway but use yarn B in place of yarn F.

FINISHING
When sewing the squares together, ease the extra stitches or extra rows into the adjoining square. Make strips as follows: 1st and 5th strips (start at bottom join) – 3A, 4B, 1B, 4A, 3B, 4A, 1A. 2nd and 6th strip (start at bottom join) – 2A, 5B, 2B, 5A, 2B, 5B, 2A. 3rd and 7th strip (start at bottom join) – 1A, 4A, 3B, 4B, 1B, 4B, 3A. 4th strip (start at bottom join) – 2A, 5A, 2B, 5B, 2B, 5A, 2A.
Join strips together to form blanket.

Edging
With RS facing and using two 3.25mm (US 3) circular needles and yarn A, pick up and knit 296 sts along the RH edge of the afghan. Beg with a WS row, cont to work in the foll garter stitch stripe patt, inc 1 st at each end of all WS rows:
ROW 1 (WS): Using yarn A, knit.
ROWS 2–3: Using yarn F, knit.
ROWS 4–5: Using yarn A, knit.
ROW 6 (RS): Using yarn F, knit.
With WS facing and using yarn F, cast (bind) off sts knitwise.
Rep for LH edge of afghan.
With RS facing and using two 3.25mm (US 3) circular needles and yarn A, pick up and knit 275 sts along bottom edge of the afghan.
Rep edging as for RH and LH edges. Rep for top edge of afghan.
Neatly sew border edges together.

Heart-to-Heart Warmers

Vibrant pinks and purples are cooled down with a hint of turquoise in this pretty, traditional Fair Isle pattern. A knitted drawstring tie at the top of each leg-warmer enables you to secure them comfortably around your legs. Your calves and ankles will never get cold.

SIZE
One size

MATERIALS
3.25mm (US 3) circular needle,
40cm (16in) long
4.00mm (US 6) circular needle,
40cm (16in) long
Pair 2.75mm (US 2) needles

Yarn
Rowan *Pure Wool DK*
50g (1¾oz) per ball
(A) 042 Dahlia	1
(B) 009 Ultramarine	2
(C) 039 Lavender	1
(D) 006 Pier	1

Extras
Beads: 160 × 4mm (⅛in)
lilac beads; 2 large, round, pink
ceramic beads; 2 large, round,
purple ceramic beads; 2 large,
square, pink ceramic beads; 2
large, square, purple ceramic
beads

TENSION (GAUGE)
26 sts and 28 rows to 10cm (4in)
measured over Fair Isle pattern
using 4.00mm (US 6) needles

KNIT
Make two leg warmers the same.

Ribbing (begin at the ankle and work up the leg)
Thread 80 beads on yarn B.
Using yarn A and 3.25mm (US 3)
circular needle, cast on 81 sts.
NEXT ROW (RS) (JOIN THE ROUND):
Using yarn A, sl the last cast-on st
on the RH needle onto the LH
needle and knit it together with the
first st, then k1, (p2, k2) 19 times,
p2. (80 sts)
Mark the first stitch of the round.
NEXT ROUND: Using yarn A, (k2, p2)
20 times.
Rep the last round 10 times more.

Leg
Change to 4.00mm (US 6) circular
needle.
Using the Fair Isle technique work
chart Rows 1–24, rep the 10-stitch
patt rep 8 times across each round.
Rep chart Rows 13–24, 4 times
more.

Ribbing
Change to 3.25mm (US 3) circular
needle.
Knit 2 rounds using yarn B.
NEXT ROUND: Using yarn B, k3,
(yfwd, k2tog, k6) 9 times, yfwd,
k2tog, k3.
Knit 2 rounds using yarn B.
NEXT ROUND: Using yarn A, knit.
NEXT ROUND: Using yarn A, (k2, p2)
20 times.
Rep the last round 11 times more.
Cast (bind) off sts in rib patt.

CHART

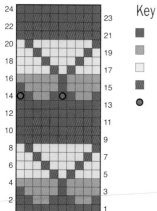

Key

- ■ B (K on RS)
- ▨ C (K on RS)
- □ D (K on RS)
- ▨ A (K on RS)
- ● Bead

Drawstring (make 2)

The drawstring is knitted by casting on stitches (using thumb method) and then casting (binding) them off. It is important that you do the following test before knitting the drawstring:

Using yarn C and 2.75mm (US 2) needle, cast on 10 sts using the thumb method.

Cast (bind) off sts.

Measure the length of the drawstring.

Each drawstring needs to be approximately 56cm (22in) long.

Calculate the number of stitches you will need for each drawstring using the following calculation:
10 sts = Xcm (Xin)
Desired length of drawstring = 56cm (22in).

METRIC CALCULATION:
56cm divided by Xcm = Y.

Y multiplied by 10 sts = the number of stitches you need to cast on.

IMPERIAL CALCULATION:
22in divided by Xin = Y.
Y multiplied by 10 sts = the number of stitches you need to cast on.

After calculating the number of stitches, cast on using the thumb method, then cast (bind) off the stitches knitwise on the next row.

FINISHING

Sew in any loose ends on the WS of the work.

Thread a drawstring through the eyelets at the top of each leg warmer. Using the photograph as a guide, thread two beads on each drawstring and then knot the ends to secure them.

Evening Delight

Diva Handbag

This small evening bag is just big enough to carry all your essentials. The long ties, with beaded loops and buttons, which will adorn any party outfit! Why not add a striking lining to make this simply irresistible?

SIZE

18cm × 15cm (7in × 6in)

MATERIALS

Pair 3.00mm (US 2–3) needles
Pair 2.25mm (US 1) needles

Yarn

Rowan *Glace Cotton*
50g (1¾oz) per ball
   829 Twilight   2

Extras

Beads: approx. 1000 × 3mm (⅛in) silver beads ("small"); approx. 4 × 5mm (³⁄₁₆) silver beads ("large"); 2 small, round shell buttons

TENSION (GAUGE)

26 sts and 42 rows to 10cm (4in) measured over beaded pattern using 3.00mm (US 2–3) needles

KNIT
Front panel

Thread 384 small silver beads on yarn.
Cast on 51 sts using 3.00mm (US 2–3) needles.
NEXT ROW (RS): Knit.
NEXT ROW (WS): Purl.
*Beg with a RS row, work Rows 1–28 from chart.
Rep chart rows 1–26.
Change to 2.25mm (US 1) needles.

NEXT ROW (RS): Knit.
Mark the centre 3 stitches of the last row.
Knit 8 more rows.
NEXT ROW (WS): Purl.
NEXT ROW (RS): K2, (pb, k1) 24 times, k1.
With WS facing, cast (bind) off sts knitwise.*

Back panel

Thread 24 small silver beads on yarn.
With RS facing and using 2.25mm (US 1) needles, pick up and knit 51 sts along cast-on edge of front panel.
NEXT ROW (WS): Knit.
NEXT ROW (RS): Knit.
NEXT ROW (WS): Purl.
NEXT ROW (RS): K2, (pb, k1) 24 times, k1.
NEXT ROW (WS): Knit.
Change to 3.00mm (US 2–3) needles.
Work 3 rows in stocking (stockinette) stitch (knit on RS; purl on WS).
Break yarn and transfer stitches back on LH needle so that the RS of the work is facing you again.
Thread 384 small silver beads on yarn.
Rejoin yarn and rep instructions for front panel from * to *.

Ties

With RS facing and using 2.25mm (US 1) needles, pick up and knit 3 sts across the centre of the front

CHART

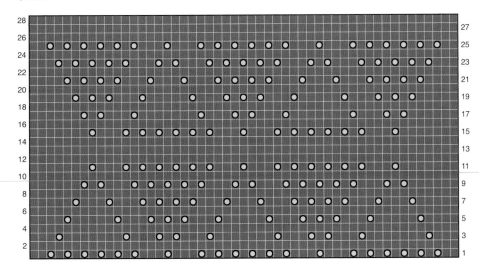

Key

■ Twighlight (K on RS)

○ Bead

panel (these are the 3 stitches that were marked earlier on).
NEXT ROW (WS): K1, p1, k1.
NEXT ROW (RS): K1, p1, k1.
NEXT ROW (WS): K1, p1, k1.
Rep the last 2 rows until tie measures approximately 18cm (7in).
Bind (cast) off sts knitwise.
Break yarn, leaving a tail of 20cm (8in).
**Thread beads onto tail of yarn as foll:
    14 small silver, 1 large silver, 14 small silver.
Push beads up yarn so that they sit tightly against the cast-off edge of the tie.
Using a needle, thread the end of the yarn through the bound-off edge of the tie to make a beaded loop.**
Rep from ** to ** to make a second beaded loop.

Using photograph as a guide, sew a small button on the end of each tie, positioning them just above the beaded loops.
Rep instructions for tie on the back panel.

Strap
NOTE: The length of the strap of the bag in the photograph is 43cm (17in). You can change the length if you wish by casting on more/fewer stitches to make it longer/shorter, but remember that you will also need to thread on more/fewer beads.

Thread 53 small silver beads on yarn.
Cast on 121 sts using 2.25mm (US 1) needles.
Knit 5 rows.
NEXT ROW (WS): Purl.
NEXT ROW (RS): K8, (pb, k1) to last 9 sts, pb, k8.
Knit 4 rows.
Cast (bind) off sts knitwise.

FINISHING
Sew in any loose ends on the WS of the work.
    Join side seams.
    Sew each end of strap securely and neatly on the inside of the bag at side edges, positioning it approximately 2.5cm (1in) from the top edge (so that the first and last beads sit slightly above the edge of the bag).

If you choose to line the bag, fold fabric in half with right sides together. Join with 1.5cm (½in) seams. Press 1.5cm (½in) to wrong side around opening. Turn to right side. Place inside knitted bag and slipstitch to wrong side of cast (bound) off edge.

Glitzy Sequin Purse

Sequins and beads are combined with cashmere to create this jazzy evening purse which is perfect for any special occasion. It's sophisticated yet stylish, while the back of it is knitted in a simple slipstitch pattern making this eye-catching design a quick project to make.

SIZE

Approximately 12.5cm × 9cm (5in × 3½in)

MATERIALS

Pair 2.75mm (US 2) needles
Pair 2.25mm (US 1) needles

Yarn

Rowan *Classic Cashsoft 4-ply*
50g (1¾oz) per ball
   430 Loganberry   1

Extras

Beads: 212 × 3mm (⅛in) mauve beads
Sequins: approx. 140 pink, 120 blue, 120 purple × 3mm (⁵⁄₁₆in) sequins
1 Metal antique button

TENSION (GAUGE)

35 sts and 26 rows to 10cm (4in) measured over sequin pattern using 2.75mm (US 2) needles

KNIT
Front panel

Thread beads and sequins on yarn as folls:

   72 beads, (20 pink sequins, 20 blue sequins, 20 purple sequins), 6 times, then 20 pink sequins.

Cast on 44 sts using 2.75mm (US 2) needles.
NEXT ROW (RS): Knit.
NEXT ROW (WS): Purl.
Rep the last 2 rows once more.

SEQUIN PATTERN REP:
ROW 1 (RS): K3, (ps, k1) 20 times, k1.
ROW 2 (WS): Purl.
Rep the 2 row patt rep 18 times more, ending with a WS row (this will use up all of the sequins).
NEXT ROW (RS): Knit.
NEXT ROW (WS) (DECREASE): P21, p2tog, p21. (43 sts)
Change to 2.25mm (US 1) needles.

BEAD PATTERN REP:
ROW 1 (RS): K2, (pb, k1) 9 times, k4, (pb, k1) 9 times, k1.
ROW 2 (WS): Purl.
Rep the 2 row patt rep twice more, ending with a WS row.
NEXT ROW (RS): K2, (pb, k1) 9 times, k4, (pb, k1) 9 times, k1.
With WS facing cast (bind) off sts knitwise.

Back panel

Thread 80 beads onto yarn. With RS facing and using 2.25mm (US 1) needles,

pick up and knit 44 sts along cast-on edge of front panel.
NEXT ROW (WS): Knit.
Change to 2.75mm (US 2) needles.
NEXT ROW (RS): Knit.
NEXT ROW (WS) (DECREASE): P21, p2tog, p21. (43 sts)

SLIP ST PATTERN REP:
ROW 1 (RS): K1, (yfwd, sl 1 purlwise, yb, k1) 21 times.
ROW 2 (WS): Purl.

ROW 3 (RS): K2, (yfwd, sl 1 purlwise, yb, k1) 20 times, k1.
ROW 4 (WS): Purl.
Rep the 4-row patt rep 9 times more, ending with a WS row.
Rep patt rep rows 1–2 once more.
Change to 2.25mm (US 1) needles.

BEAD PATTERN REP:

ROW 1 (RS): K2, (pb, k1) 20 times, k1.

ROW 2 (WS): Purl.

Rep the 2-row patt rep twice more, ending with a WS row.

NEXT ROW (RS): K2, (pb, k1) 20 times, k1.

With WS facing, cast (bind) off 13 sts knitwise, purl next 17 sts, which includes the st already on RH needle, then cast (bind) off rem 13 sts knitwise.

You will have 17 sts in the centre of the back panel, remaining on the needle.

Break yarn.

For the tab fastening, thread 60 beads on yarn.

With RS facing rejoin yarn to 17 sts for tab and knit across row.

NEXT ROW (WS): K1, p15, k1.

BEAD PATTERN REP:

ROW 1 (RS): K1, (pb, k1) 8 times.

ROW 2 (WS): K1, p15, k1.

Rep the 2-row patt rep twice more, ending with a WS row.

NEXT ROW (RS) (BUTTONHOLE): K1, (pb, k1) 3 times, cast (bind) off next 3 sts, (k1, pb) 3 times, which includes the st already on RH needle, k1.

NEXT ROW (WS): K1, p6, turn work, cast on 3 sts, turn work, p6, k1.

NEXT ROW (RS): K1, (p1, k1) 3 times, k4, (pb, k1) 3 times.

NEXT ROW (WS): K1, p15, k1.

Rep rows 1–2 twice more.

Rep Row 1 once more.

With WS facing, cast (bind) off sts knitwise.

FINISHING

Sew in any loose ends on the WS of the work.

It is advisable not to press the panels because of the sequins.

Join side seams.

Sew button to front panel to correspond with buttonhole on tab.

Glitzy Sequin Scarf

Complete your outfit with this elegant scarf – the dazzling sequins are sure to set you apart from the crowds.
Easy to make and it is the perfect accompaniment for the Glitzy Sequin Purse on page 40.

SIZE

Approximately 14cm × 117cm
(5½in × 46in) excluding fringing

MATERIALS

Pair 3.00mm (US 2–3) needles
Pair 2.75mm (US 2) needles
Pair 2.25mm (US 1) needles

Yarn

Rowan *Classic Cashsoft 4-ply*
50g (1¾oz) per ball
   430 Loganberry   2

Extras

Beads: 500 blue and 498
   turquoise × 3mm (⅛in) beads
Sequins: approx. 192 pink, 144
   blue, 144 purple × 8mm (⁵⁄₁₆in)
   sequins

TENSION (GAUGE)

36 sts and 50 rows to 10cm (4in)
measured over lace pattern using
3.00mm (US 2–3) needles

NOTE: the scarf is knitted in two
separate halves, that are joined
together after knitting.

KNIT

Scarf (make 2)

Thread beads and sequins on yarn
as folls:
   25 blue beads,
   24 purple beads,
   25 blue beads,
   (24 pink sequins,
   24 blue sequins,
   24 purple sequins) 3 times
   then (24 pink sequins,
   25 purple beads,
   25 blue beads) 8 times
   then 25 purple beads.

Cast on 51 sts using 2.75mm
(US 2) needles.
NEXT ROW (RS): K1, (make beaded
loop, k2) 16 times, make beaded
loop, k1.
NEXT ROW (WS): K1, p49, k1.
NEXT ROW (RS) (DECREASE): K2,
(ps, k1) 11 times, ps, k2tog, (ps,
k1) 11 times, ps, k1. (50 sts)
NEXT ROW (WS): K1, p48, k1.

SEQUIN PATTERN REP:
ROW 1 (RS): K2, (ps, k1) 24 times.
ROW 2 (WS): K1, p48, k1.
Rep the 2 row patt rep 8 times
more, ending with a WS row (this
will use up all of the sequins).
Change to 2.25mm (US 1)
needles.

NEXT ROW (RS) (INCREASE): K24,
inc once into next st, k25. (51 sts)
NEXT ROW (WS): K1, p49, k1.

BEAD PATTERN REPEAT:
ROW 1 (RS): K1, (pb, k1) 25 times.
ROW 2 (WS): K1, p49, k1.
ROW 3 (RS): K2, (pb, k1) 24 times,
k1.
ROW 4 (WS): K1, p49, k1.
ROWS 5–6: Rep rows 1–2.
Change to 3.00mm (US 2–3)
needles.

LACE PATTERN REPEAT:
*ROW 1 (RS): P1, (yb, sl 1 purlwise,
yfwd, p3) to last 2 sts, yb, sl 1
purlwise, yfwd, p1.
ROW 2 (WS): K1, (p1, k3) to last 2
sts, p1, k1.

ROW 3 (RS): P1, (yb, sl 1 purlwise, yfwd, p1, yon, p2tog) to last 2 sts, yb, sl 1 purlwise, yfwd, p1.
ROW 4 (WS): As Row 2.
ROW 5 (RS): As Row 1.
Change to 2.75mm (US 2) needles.
ROW 6 (WS): K1, p49, k1.
ROWS 7–9: Knit.
ROW 10 (WS): K1, p49, k1.
Change to 3.00mm (US 2–3) needles.*
Rep from * to * until scarf is half the desired length, finishing after having completed row 7.
Leave sts on a holder.

FINISHING
Sew in any loose ends on the WS of the work.

With WS facing and using a pressing cloth, lightly press the panels, taking care to exclude the sequins from the pressing.

Join the two halves of the scarf by holding WS facing and casting (binding) off the sts together using a third needle.

Smooth operator

During wear the sequins might flick up and turn the other way, so take care to check them regularly and smooth them down again if necessary.

Superstar Belt

Wow all your friends with this star-studded belt – which looks just as good worn over a slinky evening dress as it does with a pair of jeans. The buttons and long beaded tassels at each end encourage it to drape elegantly down from the hips or waist. Now you can be a superstar any night of the week!

SIZE

Approximately 3.5cm (1⅜in) wide; and the desired length to suit your individual size.

MATERIALS

Pair 3.00mm (US 2–3) needles

Yarn

Rowan *Wool Cotton*
50g (1¾oz) per ball
956 Coffee Rich   2

Extras

Beads: approx. 1020 silver and 210 pearl × 3mm (⅛in) beads
20 Star-shaped pearl buttons

TENSION (GAUGE)

32 sts and 52 rows to 10cm (4in) measured over beaded patt using 3.00mm (US 2–3) needles.

SPECIAL ABBREVIATION

make beaded loop = Knit next st leaving st on LH, slide 43 beads up the yarn so that they are sitting close to the needle and wrap the yarn with 43 beads round thumb of either hand to make a loop, take yarn between the needles to back of work and knit same st again, this time slipping st off LH needle. Lift the extra st just made over this loop and off the needle.

NOTE: The belt is knitted in two separate halves, which are joined together after knitting. The stitches determine the width of the belt and the rows determine the length of it.

KNIT
Belt (make 2)

Thread beads on yarn in the foll sequence:

    *(1 silver, 1 pearl) 21 times,
    1 silver*.

Rep from * to *, 4 times more, then thread on 400 silver beads (this is a minimum), then *(1 silver, 1 pearl) 21 times, 1 silver*. Rep from * to * 4 times more..

Cast on 11 sts using 3.00mm (US 2–3) needles.
ROW 1 (RS): K1, (make beaded loop, k1) 5 times, k1.
ROW 2 (WS): Purl.
ROW 3 (RS): K5, pb, k5.
ROW 4 (WS): Purl.
ROW 5 (RS): Knit.
ROW 6 (WS): P1, k9, p1.
ROW 7 (RS): Knit.
ROW 8 (WS): Purl.
ROW 9 (RS): K1, (pb, k1) 5 times.
ROW 10 (WS): P1, k9, p1.
ROW 11 (RS): Knit.
ROW 12 (WS): Purl.
ROW 13 (RS): Knit.
ROW 14 (WS): Purl.
Rep rows 3–14, 3 times more.

Rep rows 3–6 once more.

BEAD PATTERN REP:
ROW 1 (RS): Knit.
ROW 2 (WS): Purl.
ROW 3 (RS): K1, (pb, k1) 5 times.
ROW 4 (WS): P1, k9, p1.
Rep the 4-row beaded patt rep until the belt is half the desired length, finishing after having completed Row 3.
Thread on more beads if needed. Leave sts on a holder.

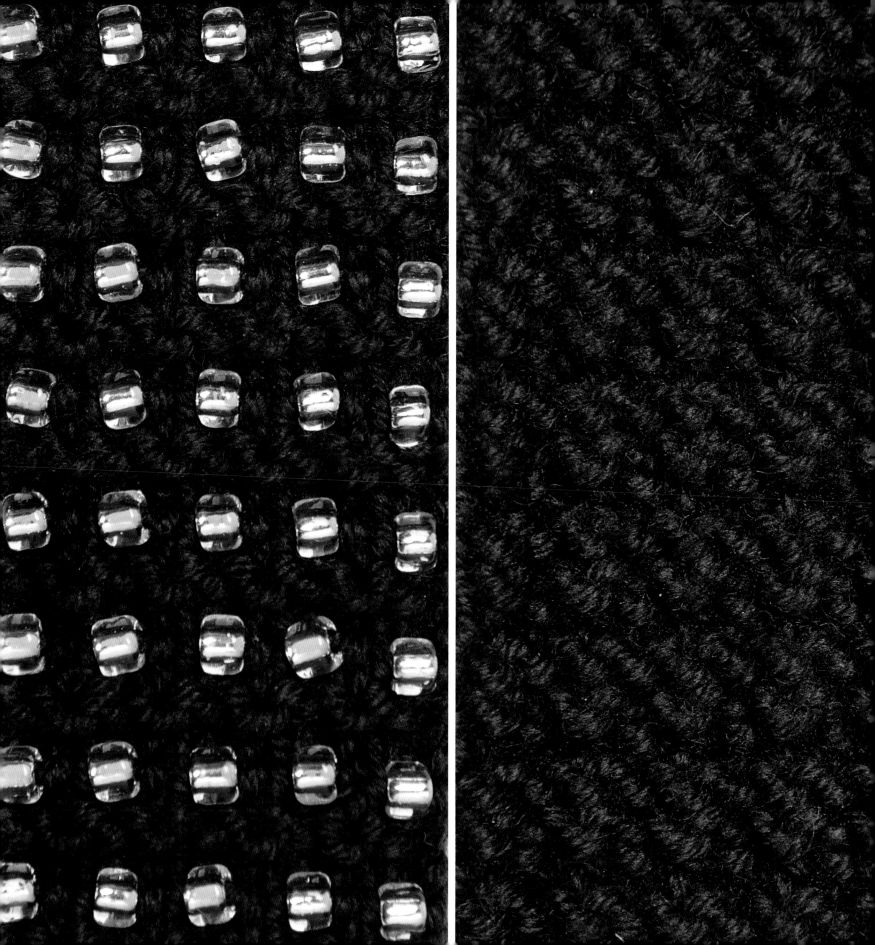

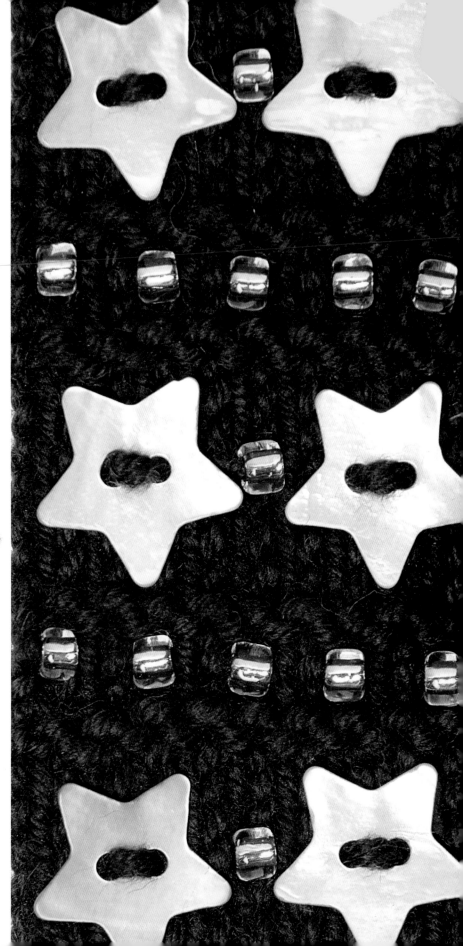

FINISHING

Sew in any loose ends on the WS
of the work.

Join the two halves of the belt by
holding WS facing and casting
(binding) off the sts together using
a third needle.

Using photograph as a guide, sew
10 buttons on each end of the
belt.

Waisting time...

To work out a suitable length of the belt for you, tie a piece of
ribbon around your waist with an overhang at each end of
approximately 40cm (16in). Measure the length of the ribbon
and divide by two, making two pieces the same length.

Lola Headband

Encrusted with beads, buttons and textured stitches, Lola can be worn to accessorize or simply complement your attire. It will look just as good worn casually with jeans and a sweater. Quick and easy to knit, you could use up your yarn stash and make several of them in a jiffy.

SIZE
One size

MATERIALS
Pair 3.00mm (US 2–3) needles
Pair 3.25mm (US 3) needles

Yarn
(Colourway 1)
Rowan *Pure Wool DK*
50g (1¾oz) per ball
039 Lavender   1

(Colourway 2)
Rowan *Pure Wool DK*
50g (1¾oz) per ball
026 Hyacinth   1

Extras
(Colourway 1)
Beads (3mm/⅛in): 119 mauve beads (A), 72 beads in mixed blues and purples (B)
Beads (5mm/³⁄₁₆in): 6 blue beads (C) ("large blue")
6 Round blue shell buttons, medium size
6 Round lilac shell buttons, medium size

(Colourway 2)
Beads (3mm/⅛in): 119 pink beads (A), 72 beads in mixed pinks and reds (B)

Beads (5mm/³⁄₁₆in): 6 red beads (C) ("large red")
6 Round shell buttons, medium size
6 Square shell buttons, medium size

TENSION (GAUGE)
28 sts and 42 rows to 10cm (4in) measured over beaded patt using 3.25mm (US 3) needles.
NOTE: Colourway 1 is knitted with a tie fastening that can be adjusted to suit. Colourway 2 is knitted as a complete band without ties.

(Colourway 1)
Thread beads on yarn in the foll sequence:
      (17 mauve, 6 mixed blues and purples, 1 large blue, 6 mixed blues and purples) 6 times, 17 mauve.

(Colourway 2)
Thread beads on yarn in the foll sequence:
      (17 pink, 6 mixed pinks and reds, 1 large red, 6 mixed pinks and reds) 6 times, 17 pink.

(Colourway 1)
Cast on 5 sts using 3.00mm (US 2–3) needles.
Beg with a RS row, work in stocking (stockinette) stitch (knit on RS rows; purl on WS rows); work until

tie measures 15cm (6in), ending with a WS row.
NEXT ROW (RS) (INCREASE): Inc once into each of the first 4 sts, k1. (9 sts)
NEXT ROW (WS): Purl.
NEXT ROW (RS) (INCREASE): K1, (inc once into next st, k1) 4 times. (13 sts)
NEXT ROW (WS): K1, (p1, k1) 6 times.
Work 6 more rows in moss (seed) stitch as set by previous row.
NEXT ROW (RS): Knit.
NEXT ROW (WS): K1, p11, k1.

(Colourway 2)
Cast on 7 sts using 3.00mm (US 2–3) needles.
NEXT ROW (RS): K1, (p1, k1) 3 times.
NEXT ROW (WS): K1, (p1, k1) 3 times.
Rep the last 2 rows, 3 times more.
NEXT ROW (RS) (INCREASE): Inc once into each of the first 6 sts, k1. (13 sts)
NEXT ROW (WS): K1, p11, k1.

BEAD PATTERN REP:
(Both colourways)
*Change to 3.25mm (US 3) needles.
ROW 1 (RS): K1, (pbA, k1) 6 times.
ROW 2 (WS): K1, p11, k1.
ROW 3 (RS): K2, (pbA, k1) 5 times, k1.
ROW 4 (WS): K1, p11, k1.
ROWS 5–6: As rows 1–2.
Change to 3.00mm (US 2–3) needles.
ROW 7 (RS): K1, (p1, k1) 6 times.
ROW 8 (WS): K1, (p1, k1) 6 times.
ROWS 9–12: Rep Rows 7–8 twice.
Change to 3.25mm (US 3) needles.
ROW 13 (RS): Knit.

ROW 14 (WS): K1, p11, k1.
ROW 15 (RS): K1, (pbB, k1) 6 times.
ROW 16 (WS): K1, p11, k1.
ROWS 17–18: Rep Rows 13–14.
ROW 19 (RS): K6, pbC, k6.
ROW 20 (WS): K1, p11, k1.
ROWS 21–22: Rep Rows 13–14.
ROWS 23–24: Rep Rows 15–16.
Change to 3.00mm (US 2–3) needles.
ROW 25 (RS): K1, (p1, k1) 6 times.
ROW 26 (WS): K1, (p1, k1) 6 times.
ROWS 27–30: Rep Rows 25–26 twice.
Change to 3.25mm (US 3) needles.
ROWS 31–32: Rep Rows 13–14.*
Rep from * to * 5 times more.

(Colourway 1)
Rep Rows 1–12.
NEXT ROW (RS) (DECREASE): K1, (k2tog, k1) 4 times. (9 sts)
NEXT ROW (WS): Purl.
NEXT ROW (RS) (DECREASE): K1, (k2tog) 4 times. (5 sts)
NEXT ROW (WS): Purl.
Change to 3.00mm (US 2–3) needles.
Beg with a RS row, work in stocking (stockinette) stitch (knit on RS rows, purl on WS rows), work until tie measures 6in (15cm), ending with a WS row.
With RS facing cast (bind) off sts knitwise.

(Colourway 2)
Rep rows 1–6.
Change to 3.00mm (US 2–3) needles.
NEXT ROW (RS) (DECREASE): K1, (k2tog) 6 times. (7 sts)
NEXT ROW (WS): K1, (p1, k1) 3 times.

NEXT ROW (RS): K1, (p1, k1) 3 times.
Rep the last 2 rows, 3 times more.
With WS facing cast (bind) off sts purlwise.

FINISHING
Sew in any loose ends on the WS of the work.
With WS facing and using a pressing cloth, lightly press the headband.

Using photograph as a guide, sew buttons to headband.
Colourway 2 only: Sew cast-on edge to cast-off edge to join band.

Bolero jacket

This handsome bolero jacket boasts an Inca-inspired two-colour beaded edging. A fancy tie detail spruces up the neckline and the simple box shape married short sleeves and decorative buttons give it a special finish that's simply to die for!

SIZE

To fit bust

XS	S	M	L	XL	
81	86	91	97	102	cm
32	34	36	38	40	in

Actual width

42.5	44.5	47.5	49.5	52.5	cm
16½	17½	18½	19½	20½	in

Length to shoulder

35	35	36	36	37	cm
13½	13½	14	14	14½	in

Sleeve length

16	16	16	16	16	cm
6½	6½	6½	6½	6½	in

MATERIALS

Pair 3.25mm (US 3) needles
Pair 2.75mm (US 2) needles
One 2.75mm (US 2) circular
   needle 40cm (16in) long

Yarn

Rowan *4-ply Soft*
50g (1¾oz) per ball
   389 Expresso

XS	S	M	L	XL
6	6	6	7	7

Extras

Beads (¹⁄₁₆in/2mm), gold: XS =
   1,550, S = 1,600, M = 1,650,
   L = 1, 700, XL = 1,750
Beads (³⁄₁₆in/5mm), triangular,
   green: XS = 56, S = 56, M =
   56, I = 56, XL = 56
Round shell buttons: XS = 6,
   S = 6, M = 6, L = 6, XL = 6

TENSION (GAUGE)

28 sts and 36 rows to 10cm (4in)
measured over stocking
(stockinette) stitch using 3.25mm
(US 3) needles

KNIT
Back panel

*NOTE: Omit beads on the first
and last sts of rows throughout the
beaded pattern.
Thread beads onto yarn in the
correct sequence, reading beads
from chart for back panel as foll:
beg at the top of the chart (chart
Row 24) on the left-hand side, and
starting and finishing between the
correct lines for your size, read
across the row from left to right.
Move to the next row down on the
chart (chart Row 22) and read
across chart as before from left to
right. Cont to read the chart in this
way, threading beads onto yarn in
the correct order.*

Cast on 119 (125: 133: 139: 147)
sts using 2.75mm (US 2) needles.
NEXT ROW (RS): Knit.
NEXT ROW (WS): Knit.
Rep the last 2 rows once more.
Change to 3.25mm (US 3)
needles.
Beg with a RS row and Row 1 of
the chart for back panel, work until
chart Row 24 completed.
Cont to work straight in stocking
(stockinette) stitch (knit on RS
rows; purl on WS rows), until back
panel measures 16cm (6½in) from
cast-on edge.

SHAPE ARMHOLES

Cast (bind) off 5 (6: 6: 7: 7) sts at beg of next 2 rows.

[109 (113: 121: 125: 133) sts]

NEXT ROW (RS) (DECREASE): K3, sl 2, k1, p2sso, K to last 6 sts, k3tog, k3.

NEXT ROW (WS): Purl.

Rep the last 2 rows 1 (1: 2: 2: 3) times more.

NEXT ROW (RS) (DECREASE): K3, sl 1, k1, psso, K to last 5 sts, k2tog, k3.

NEXT ROW (WS): Purl.

Rep the last 2 rows 3 (4: 4: 5: 5) times more.

Work 2 rows in stocking (stockinette) stitch, ending with a WS row.

NEXT ROW (RS) (DECREASE): K3, sl 1, k1, psso, K to last 5 sts, k2tog, k3.

[91 (93: 97: 99: 103) sts]

Cont straight until armhole measures 19 (19: 20: 20: 21) cm, ending with a WS row.

SHAPE SHOULDERS AND BACK NECK

Cast off 5 (5: 6: 6: 6) sts at beg of next 2 rows.

[81 (83: 85: 87: 91) sts]

NEXT ROW (RS): Cast off 5 (5: 6: 6: 6) sts, knit until there are 9 (9: 9: 9: 11) sts on right needle and turn, leaving rem sts on a holder.

Work each side of neck separately.

Cast off 4 sts at beg of next row.

Cast off rem 5 (5: 5: 5: 7) sts.

With RS facing rejoin yarn to rem sts, bind off centre 53 (55: 55: 57: 57) sts, knit to end.

Complete to match first side, reversing shapings.

Left front

Rep instructions for threading beads for back panel from * to *, but work from chart for left front.

Cast on 59 (62: 66: 69: 73) sts using 2.75mm (US 2) needles.

NEXT ROW (RS): Knit.

NEXT ROW (WS): Knit.

Rep the last 2 rows once more.

Change to 3.25mm (US 3) needles.

Beg with a RS row and Row 1 of the chart for left front, work until chart Row 24 completed.

Cont to work straight in stocking (stockinette) stitch (knit on RS rows; purl on WS rows), until left front matches back panel to beg armhole shaping.

SHAPE ARMHOLE

Cast (bind) off 5 (6: 6: 7: 7) sts at beg of next row.

[54 (56: 60: 62: 66) sts]

NEXT ROW (WS): Purl.

NEXT ROW (RS) (DECREASE): K3, sl 2, k1, p2sso, K to end.

NEXT ROW (WS): Purl.

Rep the last 2 rows 1 (1: 2: 2: 3) times more.

NEXT ROW (RS) (DECREASE): K3, sl 1, k1, psso, K to end.

NEXT ROW (WS): Purl.

Rep the last 2 rows 3 (4: 4: 5: 5) times more.

Work 2 rows in stocking (stockinette) stitch, ending with a WS row.

NEXT ROW (RS) (DECREASE): K3, sl 1, k1, psso, K to end.

[45 (46: 48: 49: 51) sts]

Cont straight until 13 (13: 13: 15: 15) rows less have been worked than on back to beg of shoulder shaping, ending with a RS row.

SHAPE FRONT NECK

Cast (bind) off 11 (12: 12: 12: 12) sts at beg of next row and 7 sts at beg of foll 2 alt rows.

[20 (20: 22: 23: 25) sts]

NEXT ROW (RS) (DECREASE): K to last 6 sts, k3tog, k3.

NEXT ROW (WS): Purl.

NEXT ROW (RS) (DECREASE): K to last 5 sts, k2tog, k3.

NEXT ROW (WS): Purl.

Rep the last 2 rows 2 (2: 2: 3: 3) times more, ending with a WS row.

[15 (15: 17: 17: 19) sts]

SHAPE SHOULDER

Cast (bind) off 5 (5: 6: 6: 6) sts at beg of next and foll alt row.

Work 1 row.

Cast (bind) off rem 5 (5: 5: 5: 7) sts.

Right front

Rep instructions for threading beads for back panel from * to *, but work from chart for right front.

Cast on 59 (62: 66: 69: 73) sts using 2.75mm (US 2) needles.

NEXT ROW (RS): Knit.

NEXT ROW (WS): Knit.

Rep the last 2 rows once more.

Change to 3.25mm (US 3) needles.

Beg with a RS row and Row 1 of the chart for right front, work until chart Row 24 completed.

Complete to match left front, reversing shapings.

Sleeves (make 2)

Rep instructions for threading beads for back panel from * to *, but work from chart for sleeve.

Cast on 79 (81: 85: 87: 91) sts using 2.75mm (US 2) needles.

NEXT ROW (RS): Knit.

NEXT ROW (WS): Knit.

Rep the last 2 rows once more.

Change to 3.25mm (US 3) needles.

Beg with a RS row and row 1 of the chart for sleeve, work until chart Row 18 completed.

CHART ROW 19 (RS) (INCREASE): K3, M1, patt across chart to last 3 sts, M1, k3.

Cont to work chart rows 20–24, ending with a WS row.

NEXT ROW (RS) (INCREASE): K3, M1, knit to last 3 sts, M1.

[83 (85: 89: 91: 95) sts]

NEXT ROW (WS): Purl.

Cont to work in stocking (stockinette) stitch (knit on RS rows; purl on WS rows), inc 1 st as before at each side of 5th and every foll 6th row until there are 91 (93: 97: 99: 103) sts.

Cont straight until sleeve measures 16cm (6½in), ending with a WS row.

SHAPE TOP

Cast (bind) off 5 (6: 6: 7: 7) sts at beg of next 2 rows.

[81 (81: 85: 85: 89) sts]

NEXT ROW (RS) (DECREASE): K3, sl 2, k1, p2sso, K to last 6 sts, k3tog, k3.

NEXT ROW (WS): Purl.

Rep the last 2 rows once more.

NEXT ROW (RS) (DECREASE): K3, sl 1, k1, psso, K to last 5 sts, k2tog, k3.

NEXT ROW (WS): Purl.

Rep the last 2 rows, 4 times more.

Work 2 rows.

NEXT ROW (RS) (DECREASE): K3, sl 1, k1, psso, K to last 5 sts, k2tog, k3.

Work 3 rows.

Rep the last 4 rows, 4 times more.

BACK PANEL

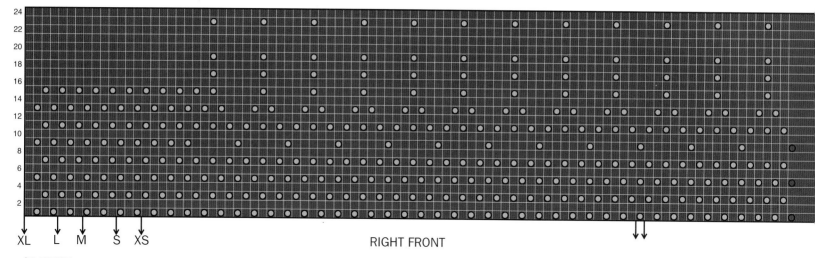

XL   L   M   S   XS   RIGHT FRONT

SLEEVE

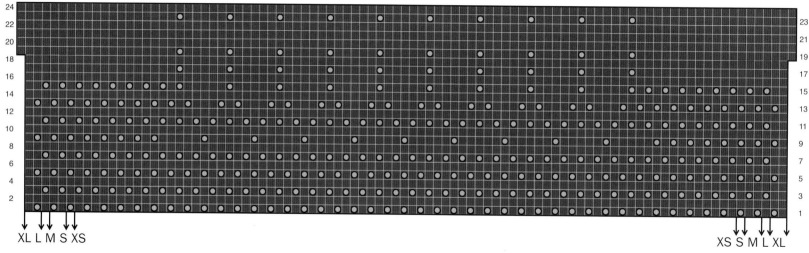

XL L M S XS   XS S M L XL

NEXT ROW (RS) (DECREASE): K3, sl 1, k1, psso, K to last 5 sts, k2tog, k3.
Work 1 row.
[51 (51: 55: 55: 59) sts]
Rep the last 2 rows until 43 sts rem.
NEXT ROW (RS) (DECREASE): K3, sl 2, k1, psso, K to last 6 sts, k3tog, k3.
NEXT ROW (WS): Purl.
Rep the last 2 rows twice more.
NEXT ROW (RS) (DECREASE): K3, sl 1, k1, psso, K to last 5 sts, k2tog, k3.

Work 1 row.
Cast (bind) off rem 29 sts.

FINISHING

Sew in any loose ends on the WS of the work.
With WS facing and using a pressing cloth, lightly press the panels.
Join both shoulder seams.

Left front band

With RS facing and using 2.75mm (US 2) needles, pick up and knit 93 (93: 96: 96: 99) sts down left front opening edge between neck shaping and lower edge of body, or as many sts are required for the sts to sit evenly.
Beg with a WS row, knit 3 rows (garter stitch).
With WS facing, cast (bind) off sts knitwise.

Right front band

Rep instructions for left front band but pick up sts up right front opening between lower edge of body and neck shaping.

Neckband

With RS facing and using 2.75mm (US 2) needles, and starting and ending at front opening edges, pick up and knit 4 sts across top of right front band, 36 (37: 37: 39: 39) sts up right side of neck, 61 (63: 63: 65: 65) sts from back, 36

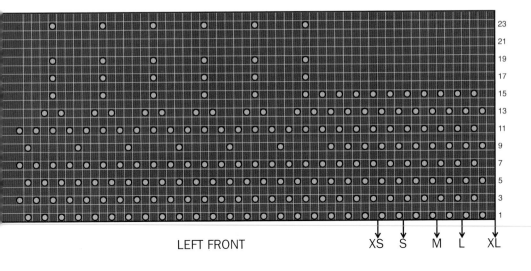

						23
						21
						19
						17
						15
						13
						11
						9
						7
						5
						3
						1

LEFT FRONT   XS   S   M   L   XL

Key

- ▪ Expresso (K on RS)
- ◉ Green bead
- ◎ Gold bead

(37: 37: 39: 39) sts down left side of neck and 4 sts across top of left front band.
[141 (145: 145: 151: 151) sts, or as many sts are required for the sts to sit evenly.]
Beg with a WS row, knit 3 rows (garter stitch).
With WS facing, cast (bind) off sts knitwise.

Join side seams of back and front panels, starting at top of beaded edging (chart Row 24) to form vents.
Join sleeve seams starting at top of beaded edging (chart Row 24), to form vents.
Set sleeves into armholes, matching the centre of cast-off edge to shoulder seams.

Vent edgings on body
(same on both sides)
*With RS facing and using 2.75mm (US 2) circular needle, pick up and knit 21 sts up one side of vent and 21 sts down other side of vent, or as many sts are required for the sts to sit evenly.
Cast (bind) off sts knitwise.*

Vent edgings on sleeve
(same on both sides)
Rep instructions for vent edgings on body from * to *.

Beaded tie 1
Thread beads on yarn as foll:
    40 gold,
    8 green.
*Using 2.75mm (US 2) needles and thumb method, work beaded cast-on as foll: cast on 2 sts leaving beads at ball side of these sts, **slide bead up yarn so that it is sitting against the needle, cast on another st making sure that the

bead is pushed to the RS of the work (facing away from you) as you put the loop onto the needle, cast on 2 sts without beads** rep from ** to **, until 1 bead rems.
Slide last bead up yarn so that it is sitting against the needle, cast on another st making sure that the bead is pushed to the RS of the work (facing away from you) as you put the loop onto the needle.
With WS facing, cast (bind) off sts knitwise.*

Beaded tie 2
Thread beads onto yarn as foll:
    8 green,
    40 gold.
Rep instructions for beaded tie 1 from * to *.

Sew ties to neck edge at front opening – one at each side with the gold beads closest to neck edge.
Using photograph as a guide, sew buttons to the body and sleeves, positioning one at the top of each of the vents and one at each side of the neck edge where the ties are attached.

Kids Out to Play

Candy Phone Cosies

With colours inspired by confectionary, plus beads for a hint of glamour, these delightful cosies will keep your mobile phone safe and clean. There are seven different designs to try out, so you could have a different phone cosy for every day of the week. You could give them away as gifts to your friends – they would make a fantastic present for both kids and adults.

SIZE
Approximately 7cm × 12cm (2½in × 4½in), excluding flap

MATERIALS
Pair 2.25mm (US 1) needles
Pair 3.00mm (US 2–3) needles

Yarn
Rowan *Cotton Glace*
50g (1¾oz) per ball
   (A) 825 Buttercup   1
   (B) 819 In the pink   1
   (C) 809 Pier   1

NOTE: this quantity of yarn is enough to knit all of the cosies.

Extras
(Candy 1)
Beads: 72 × 3mm (⅛in) blue
   beads
1 Pearl press stud

(Candy 2)
Beads: 82 × 3mm (⅛in) blue
   beads
1 Pearl press stud

(Candy 3)
Beads: 72 × 3mm (⅛in) blue
   beads
1 Small, round, shell button

(Candy Heart)
Beads: 80 × 3mm (⅛in) blue
   beads
1 Small, round, shell button

(Candy Star)
Beads: 74 × 3mm (⅛in) blue
   beads
1 Small, round, shell button

TENSION (GAUGE)
26 sts and 36 rows to 10cm (4in) measured over stocking (stockinette) stitch using 3.00mm (US 2–3) needles

KNIT
Candy 1
Front panel
Thread beads onto yarns as folls:
   yarn A: 9 beads
   yarn B: 18 beads
   yarn C: 9 beads.
Using yarn A and 3.00mm (US 2–3) needles, cast on 21 sts.
*ROW 1 (RS): Using yarn A, knit.
ROW 2 (WS): Using yarn A, purl.
ROWS 3–4: Rep Rows 1–2.
ROW 5 (RS): Using yarn A, knit.
ROW 6 (WS): Using yarn B, purl.
ROW 7 (RS): Using yarn B, knit.
ROW 8 (WS): Using yarn B, purl.
ROW 9 (RS): Using yarn B, k2 (pb, k1) 9 times, K1.
ROW 10 (WS): Using yarn B, purl.

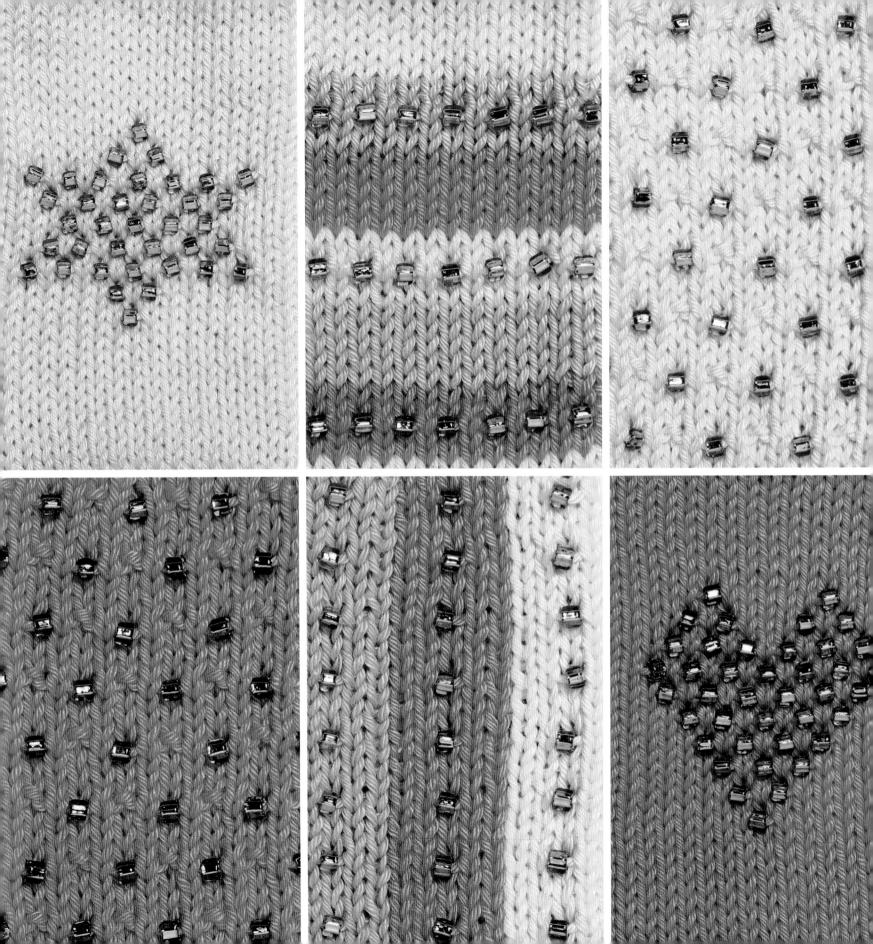

CHARTS FOR COSIES

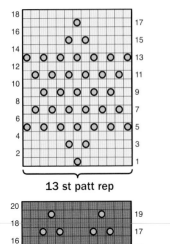

13 st patt rep

☐ A (K on RS)

○ Bead

☐ B (K on RS)

○ Bead

13 st patt rep

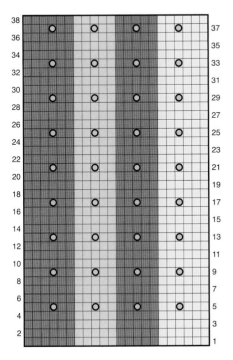

☐ A (K on RS)

▨ B (K on RS)

☐ C (K on RS)

○ Bead

ROWS 11–15: Rep Rows 1–5 using yarn C.
ROWS 16–20: Rep Rows 6–10 using yarn A.
ROWS 21–25: Rep Rows 1–5 using yarn B.
ROWS 26–30: Rep Rows 6–10 using yarn C.
ROWS 31–35: Rep Rows 1–5 using yarn A.
ROWS 36–40: Rep Rows 6–10 using yarn B.
Change to 2.25mm (US 1) needles and cont using yarn C only.
NEXT ROW (RS) (DECREASE): K10, k2tog, k9. (20 sts).
NEXT ROW (WS): K1, (p1, k1) 9 times, p1.
NEXT ROW (RS): P1, (k1, p1) 9 times, k1.
Rep the last 2 rows twice more.
With WS facing and using yarn C, cast (bind) off sts knitwise.*

Back panel
Thread beads on yarns as foll:
    yarn A: 9 beads
    yarn B: 18 beads
    yarn C: 9 beads.
With RS facing and using 2.25mm (US 1) needles and yarn C, pick up and knit 21 sts along cast on edge of front panel.
NEXT ROW (WS): Using yarn C, knit.
Change to 3.00mm (US 2–3) needles.
Rep instructions for front panel from from * to *.

Candy 2 – colourway 1
Front panel
Thread 41 beads on yarn C.
Using 3.00mm (US 2–3) needles and yarn C, cast on 21 sts.
**ROW 1 (RS): Using yarn C, knit.
ROW 2 (WS): Using yarn C, purl.
ROWS 3–4: Rep Rows 1–2.

ROW 5 (RS): Using yarn C, k2, (pb, k1, p1, k1) 4 times, pb, k2.
ROW 6 (WS): Using yarn C, purl.
ROWS 7–8: Rep Rows 1–2.
ROW 9 (RS): Using yarn C, k2, (p1, k1, pb, k1) 4 times, p1, k2.
ROW 10 (WS): Using yarn C, purl.
ROWS 11–34: Rep Rows 3–10, 3 times.
ROWS 35–37: Rep Rows 3–5.
ROW 38 (WS) (DECREASE): Using yarn C, p9, p2tog, p10. (20 sts)
Change to 2.25mm (US 1) needles.
ROW 39 (RS): Using yarn A, knit.
ROW 40 (WS): Using yarn A, k1, (p1, k1) 9 times, p1.
ROW 41 (RS): Using yarn A, p1, (k1, p1) 9 times, k1.
ROW 42 (WS): Using yarn B, k1, (p1, k1) 9 times, p1.
ROW 43 (RS): Using yarn B, p1, (k1, p1) 9 times, k1.
ROW 44 (WS): As Row 42.
ROWS 45–46: Rep Rows 43–44.
ROW 47 (RS): As Row 43.
With WS facing and using yarn B, cast (bind) off sts knitwise**.

Back panel
Thread 41 beads on yarn C.
With RS facing and using 2.25mm (US 1) needles and yarn B, pick up and knit 21 sts along cast-on edge of front panel.
NEXT ROW (WS): Using yarn B, knit.
Change to 3.00mm (US 2–3) needles.
Rep instructions for front panel from from ** to **.

Candy 2 – colourway 2
Work as Candy 2, colourway 1, using B in place of C and C in place of B. A remains the same.

Candy 2 – colourway 3

Work as Candy 2, colourway 1, using A in place of C, C in place of B and B in place of A.

Candy 3

Front panel

Thread beads on yarns as folls:

    yarn A: 9 beads
    yarn B: 18 beads
    yarn C: 9 beads.

Using 3.00mm (US 2–3) needles, cast on 22 sts in the foll sequence:

    yarn B: 6 sts; yarn C: 5 sts; yarn
    B: 5 sts; and yarn A: 6 sts.

***Beg with a RS row, work chart Rows 1–38, ending with a WS row. Change to 2.25mm (US 1) needles.

NEXT ROW (RS) (DECREASE): Using yarn C, k10, k2tog, k10. (21 sts)
Knit 3 rows using yarn C (garter stitch).
Knit 1 row using yarn A.
NEXT ROW (WS) (BUTTONHOLE): Using yarn A, k10, yfwd, k2tog, k9.
Knit 3 rows using yarn B.
With WS facing and using yarn B, cast (bind) off sts knitwise ***.

Back panel

Thread beads on yarns as foll:

    yarn A: 9 beads
    yarn B: 18 beads
    yarn C: 9 beads

With RS facing and using 2.25mm (US 1) needles and yarn A, pick up and knit 22 sts along cast on edge of front panel.
NEXT ROW (WS): Using yarn A, knit. Change to 3.00mm (US 2–3) needles.
Rep instructions for front panel from *** to ***.
Knit 4 rows using yarn C (garter stitch).
Knit 2 rows using yarn A.
Knit 3 rows using yarn B.
With WS facing and using yarn B, cast (bind) off sts knitwise.

Candy Heart

Front panel

Thread 40 beads on yarn B.
Using 3.00mm (US 2–3) needles and yarn B, cast on 21 sts.
****ROW 1 (RS): Using yarn B, knit.
ROW 2 (WS): Using yarn B, purl.
ROWS 3–12: Rep Rows 1–2, 5 times.
ROW 13 (RS): K4B, work across 13 sts of chart Row 1 for Candy Heart, k4B.
ROW 14 (WS): P4B, work across 13 sts of chart Row 2 for Candy Heart, p4B.
ROWS 15–32: Cont to work with sts as set until, until chart row 20 completed.

ROWS 33–38: Rep Rows 1–2, 3 times.
Change to 2.25mm (US 1) needles.
Knit 2 rows using yarn A (garter stitch).
Knit 3 rows using yarn C.
NEXT ROW (WS) (BUTTONHOLE): Using yarn C, k10, yfwd, k2tog, k9.
Knit 3 rows using yarn C.
With WS facing and using yarn C, cast (bind) off sts knitwise****.

Back panel

Thread 40 beads onto yarn B.
With RS facing and using 2.25mm (US 1) needles and yarn A, pick up and knit 21 sts along cast on edge of front panel.
NEXT ROW (WS): Using yarn A, knit. Change to 3.00mm (US 2–3) needles.
Rep instructions for front panel from **** to **** omitting buttonhole.

Candy Star

Front panel

Thread 37 beads onto yarn A.
Using 3.00mm (US 2–3) needles and yarn A, cast on 21 sts.
Work as Candy Heart using A in place of B, C in place of A, and B in place of C and work from chart for Candy Star.

FINISHING

For all cosies: darn in any loose ends on the WS of the work.
With WS facing and using a pressing cloth, lightly press the panels.
Sew together the side edges of the front and back panels.
Candy 1 and 2: Using photograph as a guide, attach a press stud to each cosy.
Candy 3, Candy Heart and Candy Star: Using photograph as guide, sew 1 button onto the back panel of each cosy to correspond with the buttonhole.

NOTE: The colourways shown on page 66 run as follows (from top left): Candy Star, Candy 1, Candy 2 – colourway 3, Candy 2 – colourway 1, Candy 3.

Talk of the town

These are great and fun ways to use up your left-over yarn stash. You only need a small amount!

Twinkle Jumper

This casual jumper has a useful kangaroo pocket to rest your hands in, and is given a twist with a sparkling beaded yoke. You can dress it down by wearing it with jeans, or dress it up for a party by wearing it with a pair of dress pants or a skirt. But however you decide to wear it, one thing is certain – you'll look adorable!

SIZES

1st	2nd	3rd	4th	5th	

To fit age

4–6	6–8	8–9	9–11	12–14	yrs

Actual width

41	44	47	51	53	cm
16	17½	18½	20	20½	in

Approximate length to shoulder (after washing)

45	49.5	53.5	57	60	cm
18	19½	21	22½	23½	in

Approximate sleeve length (after washing)

28	30.5	35.5	38	40.5	cm
11	12	14	15	16	in

NOTE: This yarn requires a special washing process to finish the fabric. The knitted panels will shrink in length during this wash to the correct finished measurements. See instructions at the end of this pattern for how to wash the panels.

MATERIALS

Pair 3.25mm (US 3) needles
Pair 4.00mm (US 6) needles

Yarn

Rowan *Denim*
50g (1¾oz) per ball

	1st	2nd	3rd	4th	5th
(A) 225 Nashville	6	6	7	8	9
(B) 229 Memphis	4	4	4	4	5

Extras

Beads 5mm (³⁄₁₆in):

Red	(approximate number)				
180	220	220	265	265	
Silver	(approximate number)				
365	405	405	405	445	
Pearl	(approximate number)				
205	205	250	250	250	

TENSION (GAUGE) (BEFORE WASHING)

20 sts and 28 rows to 10cm (4in) measured over stocking (stockinette) stitch using 4.00mm (US 6) needles

KNIT

Back panel

*Cast on 81 (87: 93: 101: 105) sts using yarn A and 3.25mm (US 3) needles.
NEXT ROW (RS): Using yarn A, k1, (p1, k1) to end of row.
NEXT ROW (WS): Using yarn A, k1, (p1, k1) to end of row.
Rep the last 2 rows, 4 times more.
Change to 4.00mm (US 6) needles.*
Beg with a RS row and using yarn A only, cont to work in stocking (stockinette) stitch (knit on RS rows, purl on WS rows), until work measures 38 (43: 48: 52: 56) cm from cast-on edge, ending with a WS row.

Beaded yoke

NOTE: Omit beads on the first and last sts of rows throughout the yoke.
Thread beads onto yarn B in the correct sequence, reading beads from chart for back panel as folls: beg at the top of the chart (chart Row 42) on the left-hand side, and starting and finishing between the correct lines for your size, read across the row from left to right. Move to the next row down on the chart (chart Row 40) and read across chart as before from left to right. Cont to read the chart in this way, threading beads onto yarn B in the correct order.
NEXT ROW (RS): Using yarn B, knit.
NEXT ROW (WS): Using yarn B, purl.
Beg with row 1 of the chart for back panel, and working between the correct lines for your size, cont to work beaded patt until chart row 42 completed, ending with a WS row.

SHAPE SHOULDERS AND BACK NECK

NEXT ROW (RS): Using yarn B, k25 (28: 29: 32: 34) sts and slip them onto a holder for shoulder, cast (bind) off next 31 (31: 35: 37: 37) sts, K to end and leave the rem 25 (28: 29: 32: 34) sts on another holder for shoulder.

Front panel

Rep instructions for back panel from * to *.

NEXT ROW (RS): Using yarn A, k22 (25: 28: 32: 34) sts, slip next 37 sts onto holder for pocket front, turn and cast-on 37 sts, turn and knit rem 22 (25: 28: 32: 34) sts. Beg with a WS row and using yarn A, work 43 rows in stocking (stockinette) stitch (knit on RS rows, purl on WS rows). Leave sts on a holder.

Pocket front

With RS facing, slip sts on holder for pocket front onto a needle and cont in stripe patt rep as folls:

ROW 1 (RS): Using yarn B, knit.
ROW 2 (WS): Using yarn B, purl.
ROWS 3–4: Rep Rows 1–2.
ROW 5 (RS): Using yarn A, knit.
ROW 6 (WS): Using yarn A, purl.
ROWS 7–8: Rep Rows 5–6.
Rep the 8-row patt rep 4 times more.
Rep Rows 1–4 once more.

JOIN IN POCKET

Place WS of pocket front at front of jumper front and work as folls:
With RS facing and using yarn A, K22 (25: 28: 32: 34) sts from jumper front, work across the next 37 sts of jumper front and 37 sts of pocket front together, K to end. Beg with a WS row, cont to work in stocking (stockinette) stitch (knit on RS rows; purl on WS rows)

using yarn A only, until work matches back panel to beg of beaded yoke.

Beaded yoke

NOTE: Omit beads on the first and last sts of rows throughout the yoke.

Thread beads onto yarn B in the correct sequence, reading beads from chart for front panel as folls: beg at the top of the chart (chart Row 42) on the right-hand side, and starting and finishing between the correct lines for your size, read across the row from left to right. Move to the next row down on the chart (chart Row 40) and read across chart as before from left to right. Cont to read the chart in this way, threading beads onto yarn B in the correct order.

NEXT ROW (RS): Using yarn B, knit.
NEXT ROW (WS): Using yarn B, purl.
Beg with Row 1 of the chart for front panel, and working between the correct lines for your size, cont to work beaded patt until chart row 24 (24: 22: 22: 20) completed.

SHAPE FRONT NECK

NEXT ROW (RS): K33 (36: 39: 43: 45) sts, turn leaving rem sts on a holder, work each each side separately. Dec 1 st at neck edge on next 8 (8: 10: 10: 10) rows and 0 (0: 0: 1: 1) foll alt row. 25 (28: 29: 32: 34) sts.
Cont without further shaping until chart Row 42 is completed, ending with a WS row. Leave sts on a holder for shoulder. Return to stitches on other holder and with RS facing slip centre 15 sts onto a holder, rejoin yarn and knit to end. Work as for first side, following chart for beaded pattern and reversing shaping. Leave sts on a

holder for shoulder. Break yarn. Thread beads on yarn B to complete the left-hand side and starting and finishing between the correct lines for your size, read across row from left to right as before.

Sleeves (both alike)

Cast on 39 (41: 47: 47: 47) sts using yarn A and 3.25mm (US 3) needles.

ROW 1 (RS): Using yarn A, k1, (p1, k1) to end of row.
ROW 2 (WS): Using yarn A, k1, (p1, k1) to end of row.
ROWS 3–4: Rep Rows 1–2 once.
ROW 5 (RS): Using yarn B, k1, (p1, k1) to end of row.
ROW 6 (WS): Using yarn B, k1, (p1, k1) to end of row.
ROWS 7–10: Rep Rows 5–6 twice. Change to 4.00mm (US 6) needles.
NEXT ROW (RS) (INCREASE): Using yarn A, k19 (20: 23: 23: 23) sts, inc 1, k19 (20: 23: 23: 23) sts. 40 (42: 48: 48: 48) sts.
NEXT ROW (WS): Using yarn A, purl.
NEXT ROW (RS) (INCREASE): Using yarn A, inc 1 st at beg and end of row. [42 (44: 50: 50: 50) sts]
NEXT ROW (WS): Using yarn A, purl.

Beg with a RS row, work in stripe patt rep as foll: 4 rows in stocking (stockinette) stitch (knit on RS rows; purl on WS rows) using yarn B, 4 rows in stocking (stockinette) stitch using yarn A, and at the same time inc sts at side edges as set as folls:

1ST AND 2ND SIZES ONLY: inc 1 st at each side of 3rd and every foll 4th row to 76 (80) sts.
3RD, 4TH AND 5TH SIZES ONLY: inc 1 st at each side of 3rd and 9 foll 4th rows and then every foll 6th row to 84 (88: 92) sts.

BACK AND FRONT BEADED YOKE

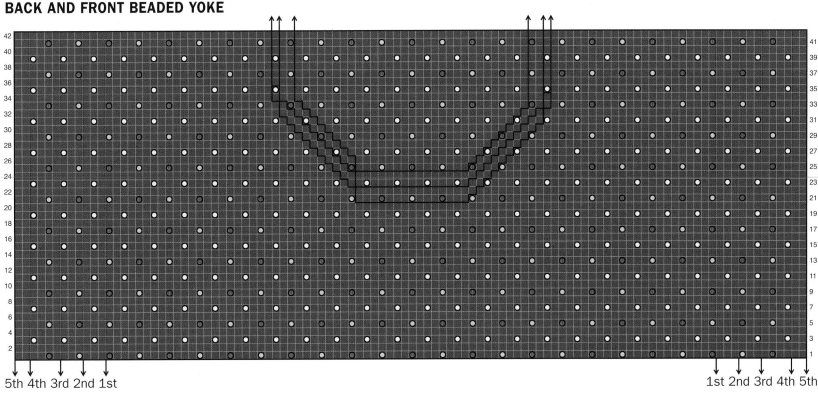

5th 4th 3rd 2nd 1st

1st 2nd 3rd 4th 5th

All sizes: Cont working straight in stripe patt rep until sleeve measures 32 (36: 40: 45: 47) cm, or length required, finishing after completing 4 rows of either yarn A or yarn B. Cast off sts loosely and evenly.

FINISHING
Darn in any loose ends on the WS of the work. Join right shoulder seam by casting off sts together on wrong side using a third needle.

Neckband
With RS facing and using yarn B and 3.25mm (US 3) needles, pick up and knit 16 (16: 18: 18: 18) sts down left side of neck, 15 sts

from front, 16 (16: 18: 18: 18) sts up right side of neck, then 31 (31: 35: 37: 37) sts from back neck. [78 (78: 86: 88: 88) sts, or as many sts are required for the sts to sit evenly.]
NEXT ROW (WS): Using yarn B, (k1, p1) to end of row.
NEXT ROW (RS): Using yarn B, (p1, k1) to end of row.
Rep the last 2 rows, 3 times more.
NEXT ROW (WS): Using yarn B, (k1, p1) to end of row.
With RS facing and using yarn B, cast (bind) off sts in moss (seed) st patt.
Join left shoulder seam by casting off sts together on wrong side using a third needle.
Join neck edging.

Pocket edging
With RS facing and using yarn A, pick up and knit 33 sts along one side (selvedge) edge of front pocket.
NEXT ROW (WS): Using yarn A, k1, (p1, k1) to end of row.
NEXT ROW (RS): Using yarn A, k1, (p1, k1) to end of row.
Rep the last 2 rows, 3 times more.
With WS facing and using yarn A, cast (bind) off sts in moss (seed) st patt. Rep for other side (selvedge) edge of front pocket.

Special washing instructions
Place the panels inside a washbag that can be secured. Wash the panels in a washing machine on the hottest setting so that shrinkage can take place.

Key

- ■ Memphis (K on RS)
- ◉ Red bead
- ◎ Silver bead
- ○ Pearl bead

Tumble dry the panels to near dryness (if facility is available).
Remove the panels from the washbag, reshape them and leave flat to dry.
When the panels are dry, complete finishing as foll:
Sew in sleeves, matching centre of bound-off edge to shoulder seams.
Join side seams and sleeve seams. Sew cast-on edge of front in place.

Rock Star Wristbands

Punk meets princess in these fun and easy-to-knit wristbands, which are a must for any young girl's wardrobe. She will be the envy of all her friends at the next party when she wears them with her latest outfit. Rock on!

SIZE (CIRCUMFERENCE OF WRISTBAND)

	S	M	L	
	16.5	18	19.5	cm
	6½	7	7½	in

MATERIALS

Pair 3.75mm (US 5) needles
Pair 3.00mm (US 2–3) needles

Yarn

Rowan *Wool Cotton*
50g (1¾oz) per ball
  (A) 911 Rich   1
  (B) 908 Inky   1
NOTE: This quantity of yarn is enough to knit all of the wristbands.

Extras

(Hearts)
Beads (3mm/⅛in), silver: S = 14, M = 16, L = 18
2 Silver press studs

(Stripes)
Beads (3mm/⅛in), silver: S = 14, M = 16, L = 18
2 Small, round, shell buttons

(Studs)
Beads (3mm/⅛in), silver: S = 82, M = 94, L = 106
2 Silver press studs

(Flower)
Beads (3mm/⅛in), silver: S = 49, M = 53, L = 57
3 Small, round, shell buttons

TENSION (GAUGE)

24 sts and 32 rows to 10cm (4in) measured over stocking (stockinette) stitch using 3.75mm (US 5) needles

KNIT
Hearts

Thread 14 (16: 18) beads on yarn A.
Using yarn A and 3.00mm (US 2–3) needles and thumb method, work beaded cast on as folls: cast on 6 sts leaving beads at ball side of these sts, *slide bead up yarn so that it is sitting against the needle, cast on another st making sure that the bead is pushed to the RS of the work (facing away from you) as you put the loop onto the needle, cast on 1 st without bead*, rep from * to * 13 (15: 17) times, cast on 5 sts.
39 (43: 47) sts.
ROW 1 (RS): Using yarn A, knit.
ROW 2 (WS): Using yarn B, k1, p4, (k1, p1) 14 (16: 18) times, k1, p4, k1.
Change to 3.75mm (US 5) needles.
ROW 3 (RS): Using yarn B, knit.
ROW 4 (WS): Using yarn B, k1, p4, k1, p27 (31: 35), k1, p4, k1.
ROW 5 (RS): Using yarn B, k14 (16: 18), work across 11 sts from chart, yarn B, k14 (16: 18).
ROW 6 (WS): Using yarn B, k1, p4, k1, p8 (10: 12), work across 11 sts from chart, yarn B, p8 (10: 12), k1, p4, k1.

ROWS 7–18: Rep Rows 5–6, 6 times.
ROWS 19–20: As Rows 3–4.
ROW 21 (RS): As Row 3.
Change to 3.00mm (US 2–3) needles.
ROW 22 (WS): Using yarn A, k1, p4, (k1, p1) 14 (16: 18) times, k1, p4, k1.
ROW 23 (RS): Using yarn A, knit. With WS facing and using yarn A, cast (bind) off sts knitwise.

Stripes

Thread 14 (16: 18) beads on yarn A.
Rep instructions for beaded cast-on for Heart, using yarn A. 39 (43: 47) sts.
ROW 1 (RS): Using yarn A, knit.
ROW 2 (WS): Using yarn B, p5, (k1, p1) 14 (16: 18) times, k1, p4, k1.
Change to 3.75mm (US 5) needles.
ROW 3 (RS): Using yarn B, knit.
ROW 4 (WS): Using yarn B, p5, k1, p27 (31: 35), k1, p2, yon, p2tog, k1.
ROW 5 (RS): Using yarn B, knit.
ROW 6 (WS): Using yarn A, p5, k1, p27 (31: 35), k1, p4, k1.
ROW 7 (RS): Using yarn A, knit.
ROWS 8–9: As Rows 6–7.
ROW 10 (WS): Using yarn B, p5, k1, p27 (31: 35), k1, p4, k1.
ROW 11 (RS): Using yarn B, knit.
ROWS 12–13: As Rows 10–11.
ROWS 14–19: Rep Rows 6–11.
ROWS 20–21: Rep Rows 4–5.
Change to 3.00mm (US 2–3) needles.

ROW 22 (WS): Using yarn A, p5, (k1, p1) 14 (16: 18) times, k1, p4, k1.
ROW 23 (RS): Using yarn A, knit. With WS facing and using yarn A, cast (bind) off sts knitwise.

Studs

Thread 82 (94: 106) beads on yarn B.
Cast on 39 (43: 47) sts using yarn B and 3.00mm (US 2–3) needles.
ROW 1 (RS): Using yarn B, knit.
ROW 2 (WS): Using yarn B, knit.
Change to 3.75mm (US 5) needles.
ROW 3 (RS): Using yarn B, knit.
ROW 4 (WS): Using yarn B, k6, p27 (31: 35) sts, k6.
ROW 5 (RS): Using yarn B, k6, (pb, k1) 14 (16: 18) times, k5.
ROW 6 (WS): As Row 4.
ROW 7 (RS): Using yarn B, k7, (pb, k1) 13 (15: 17) times, k6.
ROWS 8–9: Rep Rows 4–5.
ROW 10 (WS): Using yarn A, k1, p4, k1, p27 (31: 35) sts, k1, p4, k1.
ROW 11 (RS): Using yarn A, knit.
ROWS 12–13: Rep Rows 10–11.
ROW 14 (WS): As Row 10.
ROW 15 (RS): Using yarn B, knit.
ROW 16 (WS): As Row 4.
ROWS 17–21: Rep Rows 5–9.
Change to 3.00mm (US 2–3) needles.
ROW 22 (WS): Using yarn B, knit.
ROW 23 (RS): Using yarn B, knit. With WS facing and using yarn B, cast (bind) off sts.

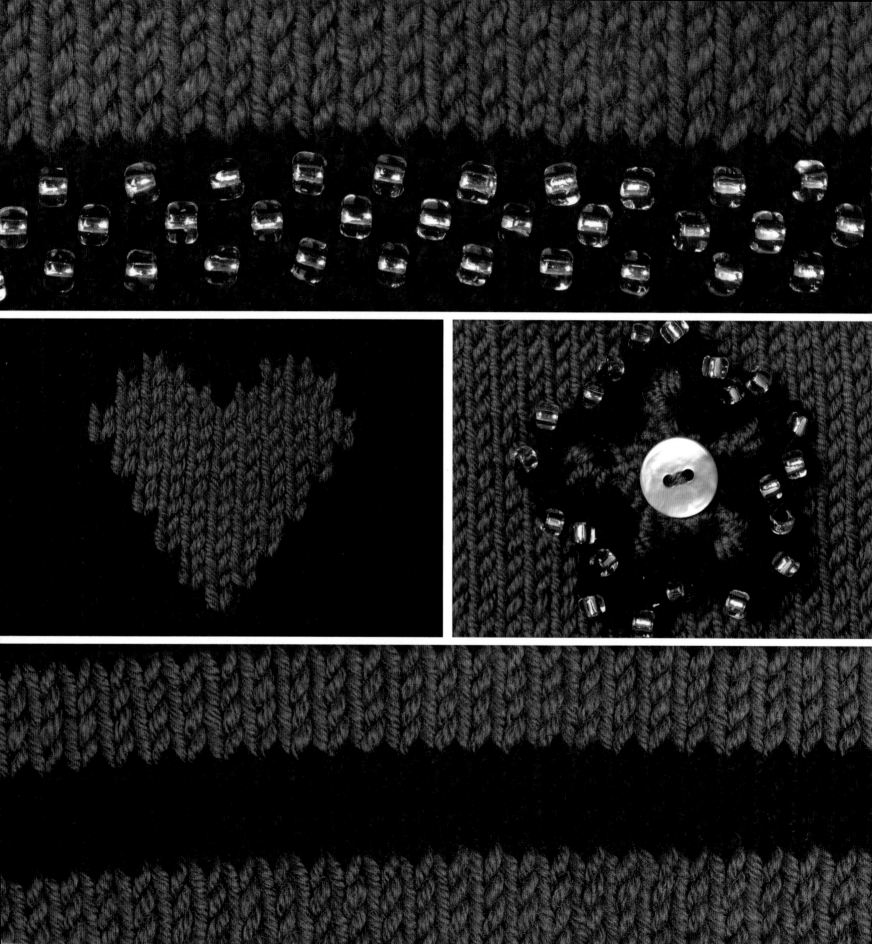

Flower

Thread 14 (16: 18) beads on yarn A and B.

Cast on 39 (43: 47) sts using yarn B and 3.00mm (US 2–3) needles.

ROW 1 (RS): Using yarn B, knit.

ROW 2 (WS): Using yarn A, k1, p4, (k1, p1) 14 (16: 18) times, k1, p4, k1.

Change to 3.75mm (US 5) needles.

ROW 3 (RS): Using yarn A, k6, (pb, k1) 14 (16: 18) times, k5.

ROW 4 (WS): Using yarn A, k1, p4, k1, p27 (31: 35), k1, p2, yon, p2tog, k1.

ROW 5 (RS): Using yarn A, knit.

ROW 6 (WS): Using yarn A, k1, p4, k1, p27 (31: 35), k1, p4, k1.

ROWS 7–18: Rep Rows 5–6, 6 times.

ROW 19 (RS): Using yarn A, knit.

ROW 20 (WS): As Row 4.

ROW 21 (RS): Using yarn A, knit.

Change to 3.00mm (US 2–3) needles.

ROW 22 (WS): Using yarn B, k1, p4, (k1, p1) 14 (16: 18) times, k1, p4, k1.

ROW 23 (RS): Using yarn B, k6, (pb, k1) 14 (16; 18) times, k5.

With WS facing and using yarn B, cast (bind) off sts knitwise.

MAKE FLOWER

Thread 21 beads on yarn B.

Using 3.00mm (US 2–3) needles, yarn B and thumb method, work beaded cast on as folls: cast-on 2 sts leaving beads at ball side of these sts, *slide bead up yarn so that it is sitting against the needle, cast on another st making sure that the bead is pushed to the RS of the work (facing away from you) as you put the loop onto the needle, cast on 1 st without bead*, rep from * to * 20 times, cast on 1 st.
(45 sts)

ROW 1 (WS): Using yarn B, purl.

ROW 2 (RS): Using yarn A, k8, sl the 2nd, 3rd, 4th, 5th, 6th, and 7th sts from the RH needle off over the 1st st, k2 (k7, sl the 2nd, 3rd, 4th, 5th, 6th and 7th sts from the RH needle off over the 1st st, k2) 3 times, k7, sl the 2nd, 3rd, 4th, 5th, 6th, and 7th sts from the RH needle off over the 1st st, k1.
(15 sts)

ROW 3 (WS): Using yarn A, knit. Break the yarn, thread it through the rem sts and pull up tightly.

FINISHING

Sew in any loose ends on the WS of the work.

With WS facing and using a pressing cloth, lightly press the wristbands.

Heart and Studs: Using photograph as a guide, attach two press studs to each wristband.

Stripes and Flower: Sew two buttons onto each wristband to correspond with the buttonholes.

Flower only: Sew a button in the centre of the flower and sew the flower to the middle of the wristband.

HEART CHART

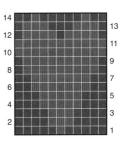

Key

A (K on RS)
B (K on RS)

Sweeties Hat

These hats are offered in three different sizes – to fit you and your child – and three slightly different styles. The single pom-pom on top of the hat makes it a fun as well as practical accessory to wear out.

SIZES

Small is to fit 18in (46cm)
Medium is to fit 20in (51cm)
Large is to fit 22in (56cm)

MATERIALS

One 3.25mm (US 3) circular
    needle, 40cm (16in) long
One 3.75mm (US 5) circular
    needle, 40cm (16in) long
Set 3.25mm (US 3) five dp needles
Set 3.75mm (US 5) five dp needles
Cable needle

Yarn

(Small size)
Rowan *Pure Wool DK*
50g (1¾oz) per ball
    (A) 036 Kiss   small amount
    (B) 019 Avocado   1

(Medium size)
Rowan *Pure Wool DK*
50g (1¾oz) per ball
    (A) 026 Hyacinth
                    small amount
    (B) 006 Pier   1
    (C) 009 Ultra-marine
                    small amount
    (D) 019 Avocado
                    small amount
    (E) 036 Kiss
                    small amount
    (F) 032 Gilt
                    small amount

(Large size)
Rowan *Pure Wool DK*
50g (1¾oz) per ball
    (A) 026 Hyacinth   2
    (B) 009 Ultra-marine
                    small amount

Extras

Beads (3mm/⅛in): S = 72 red,
    72 blue, 72 green; M = 150 red,
    75 blue, 75 green; L = 396 blue

TENSION (GAUGE)

28 sts and 36 rows to 4in (10cm)
measured over cable and bead
pattern using 3.75mm (US 5)
needles

NOTE: The pattern is written for the
small size hat, followed by the
medium size hat
in **bold** and the
large size hat in
italic.

(Small size)
Thread beads on
yarn B as folls:
    (18 blue, 18
    red, 18 green)
    4 times.

(Medium size)
Thread beads on yarn B
as foll:

(1 red bead, 1 green bead, 1
red, 1 blue) 5 times.
Rep this sequence 14 times more.

(Large size)
Thread 396 blue beads on yarn A.

KNIT

Cast on 99 (111: 123) sts using
yarn A and a circular 3.25mm (US
3) needle.
NEXT ROW (RS) (JOIN THE ROUND):
Using yarn A, slip the last cast-on
stitch onto the left-hand needle

and knit it together with the first
stitch, then (p1, k1) 48 (**54**: *60*)
times, p1. (98: **110**: *122* sts)
Mark the first stitch of the round.
NEXT ROUND: Using yarn B (**B:** *B*),
k1, (p1, k1) 48 (**54**: *60*) times, p1.
NEXT ROUND: Using yarn B (**B:** *B*),
k1, (p1, k1) 48 (**54**: *60*) times, p1.
NEXT ROUND: Using yarn B (**C:** *B*),
k1, (p1, k1) 48 (**54**: *60*) times, p1.
NEXT ROUND: Using yarn B (**C:** *A*),
k1, (p1, k1) 48 (**54**: *60*) times, p1.
NEXT ROUND: Using yarn B (**D:** *A*),
k1, (p1, k1) 48 (**54**: *60*) times, p1.
NEXT ROUND: Using yarn B (**D:** *A*),
k1, (p1, k1) 48 (**54**: *60*) times, p1.
NEXT ROUND: Using yarn B (**E:** *B*),
k1, (p1, k1) 48 (**54**: *60*) times, p1.
(Small size only)
NEXT ROUND (INCREASE): Using yarn
    B, k4, (M1, k10) 9 times, M1,
    k4. (108 sts)
        (Medium size only)
        NEXT ROUND: Using
        yarn E, k1, (p1, k1) 54
        times, p1.

NEXT ROUND: Using yarn F, k1, (p1, k1) 54 times, p1.

NEXT ROUND: Using yarn F, k1, (p1, k1) 54 times, p1.

NEXT ROUND (INCREASE): Using yarn B, k2, (M1, k11) 9 times, M1, k9. (120 sts)

(Large size only)

NEXT ROUND: Using yarn B, k1, (p1, k1) 60 times, p1.

NEXT ROUND: Using yarn B, k1, (p1, k1) 60 times, p1.

NEXT ROUND (INCREASE): Using yarn A, k7, (M1, k12) 9 times, M1, k7. (132 sts)

Change to a circular 3.75mm (US 5) needle.

ROUND 1: Using yarn B (**B**: *A*), p1, k1, (p1, k1, pb, k1, p1, k1) 17 (**19**: *21*) times, p1, k1, pb, k1.

ROUND 2 : Using yarn B (**B**: *A*), k1, p1, (k5, p1) 17 (**19**: *21*) times, k4.

ROUND 3: As Round 1.

ROUND 4: As Round 2.

ROUND 5: As Round 1.

ROUND 6: As Round 2.

ROUND 7: Using yarn B (**B**: *A*), p1, k1, (p1, c3b, p1, k1) 17 (**19**: *21*) times, p1, c3b.

ROUND 8: As Round 2.

Rep Rounds 1–8, 1 (**2**: *3*) times more.

Rep Rounds 1–7 once more.

SHAPE CROWN

NOTE: When there are too few stitches on the needle to continue knitting on the round, split the stitches onto 3.75mm (US 5) dp needles.

NEXT ROUND (DECREASE): Using yarn B (**B**: *A*), k1, (p2tog, k4) 17 (**19**: *21*) times, p2tog, k3. (90: **100**: *110* sts)

NEXT ROUND: Using yarn B (**B**: *A*), p1, (k2, pb, k1, p1) 17 (**19**: *21*) times, k2, pb, k1.

NEXT ROUND: Using yarn B (**B**: *A*), k1, (p1, k4) 17 (**19**: *21*) times, p1 k3.

NEXT ROUND: Using yarn B (**B**: *A*), p1, (k2, pb, k1, p1) 17 (**19**: *21*) times, k2, pb, k1.

NEXT ROUND (DECREASE): Using yarn B (**B**: *A*), p2tog, (k3, p2tog) 17 (**19**: *21*) times, k3. (72: **80**: *88* sts)

NEXT ROUND: Using yarn B (**B**: *A*), k2, (pb, k3) 17 (**19**: *21*) times, pb, k1.

NEXT ROUND: Using yarn B (**B**: *A*), p1, (k3, p1) 17 (**19**: *21*) times, k3.

NEXT ROUND: Using yarn B (**B**: *A*), k1, (c3b, k1) 17 (**19**: *21*) times, c3b.

NEXT ROUND (DECREASE): Using yarn B (**B**: *A*), k2tog, (k2, k2tog) 17 (**19**: *21*) times, K2. (54: **60**: *66* sts)

NEXT ROUND: Using yarn A (**A**: *B*), k54 (**60**: *66*) sts.

NEXT ROUND: Using yarn A (**A**: *B*), k54 (**60**: *66*) sts.

NEXT ROUND (DECREASE): Using yarn A (**A**: *B*), k2tog, (k4, k2tog) 8 (**9**: *10*) times, k4. (45: **50**: *55* sts)

NEXT ROUND: Using yarn B (**C**: *A*), k45 (**50**: *55*) sts.

NEXT ROUND (DECREASE): Using yarn B (**C**: *A*), k2tog, (k3, k2tog) 8 (**9**: *10*) times, k3. (36: **40**: *44* sts)

NEXT ROUND: Using yarn B (**C**: *A*), k36 (**40**: *44*) sts.

NEXT ROUND (DECREASE): Using yarn A (**A**: *B*), k2tog, (k2, k2tog) 8 (**9**: *10*) times, k2. (27: **30**: *33* sts)

NEXT ROUND: Using yarn A (**A**: *B*), k27 (**30**: *33*) sts.

NEXT ROUND (DECREASE): Using yarn A (**A**: *B*), k2tog, (k1, k2tog) 8 (**9**: *10*) times, k1. (18: **20**: *22* sts)

NEXT ROUND (DECREASE): Using yarn A (**A**: *B*), k2tog 9 (**10**: *11*) times. (9: **10**: *11* sts)

FINISHING

Run yarn through remaining stitches, draw up and fasten off.

Sew in any loose ends on the WS of the work.

Make a small pom-pom: (B for small size, C for medium size and A for large size).

Using photograph as a guide, attach pom-pom to the top of the hat.

Mind the gap

When you shape the crown and have to split the stitches onto double-pointed needles, pull the yarn firmly as you move from one needle to the next to avoid nasty gaps or ladders.

Sweeties Scarf

This scarf is designed to match the Sweeties Hat. Wear the two together and you can be sure that you'll always be found in a crowd, while your head and neck will be kept nice and warm!

SIZE
Approximately 11.5cm × 136cm (4½in × 53½in), excluding pom-poms

MATERIALS
Pair 3.75mm (US 5) needles
Cable needle

Yarn
Rowan *Pure Wool DK*
1¾oz (50g) per ball

(A) 026 Hyacinth		1
(B) 006 Pier		1
(C) 009 Ultra-marine		1
(D) 019 Avocado		1
(E) 036 Kiss		1
(F) 032 Gilt		1

Extras
Beads (3mm/⅛in): 585 red, 195 blue, 195 green

TENSION (GAUGE)
28 sts and 36 rows to 10cm (4in) measured over cable and bead pattern using 3.75mm (US 5) needles

KNIT
Thread beads on each ball of yarn for each square as foll:
  1 red bead,
  1 green bead,
  1 red bead,
  1 blue bead,
  1 red bead,
Rep this sequence 14 times more for each square. (75 beads)

Cast on 31 sts using yarn A and 3.75mm (US 5) needles.
NEXT ROW (WS): K1, p29, k1.
NEXT ROW (RS): K1, p1, (k3, p1, k1, p1) 4 times, k3, p1, k1.
NEXT ROW (WS): K1, (p5, k1) 5 times.

CABLE AND BEAD PATTERN REP:
*ROW 1 (RS): K1, p1, (k1, pb, k1, p1, k1, p1) 4 times, k1, pb, k1, p1, k1.
ROW 2 (WS): K1, (p5, k1) 5 times.
ROWS 3–6: Rep Rows 1–2 twice.
ROW 7 (RS): K1, p1, (c3b, p1, k1, p1) 4 times, c3b, p1, k1.
ROW 8 (WS): K1, (p5, k1) 5 times.
Rep Rows 1–8, three times more.
Rep Rows 1–6 once more.*

Change to yarn B.
**ROWS 39–40: Rep Rows 7–8.
ROW 41 (RS): K1, p1, (k1, pb, k1, p1, k1, p1) 4 times, k1, pb, k1, p1, k1.
ROW 42 (WS): K1, (p5, k1) 5 times.
ROWS 43–46: Rep Rows 1–2 twice.
ROW 47 (RS): K1, p1, (c3f, p1, k1, p1) 4 times, c3f, p1, k1.
ROW 48 (WS): K1, (p5, k1) 5 times.
Rep Rows 41–48, three times more.
Rep Rows 41–46, once more.**

Change to yarn C.
Rep Rows 47–48 once.
Rep from * to *.
Change to yarn D.
Rep from ** to **.
Change to yarn E.
Rep Rows 47–48 once.
Rep from * to *.

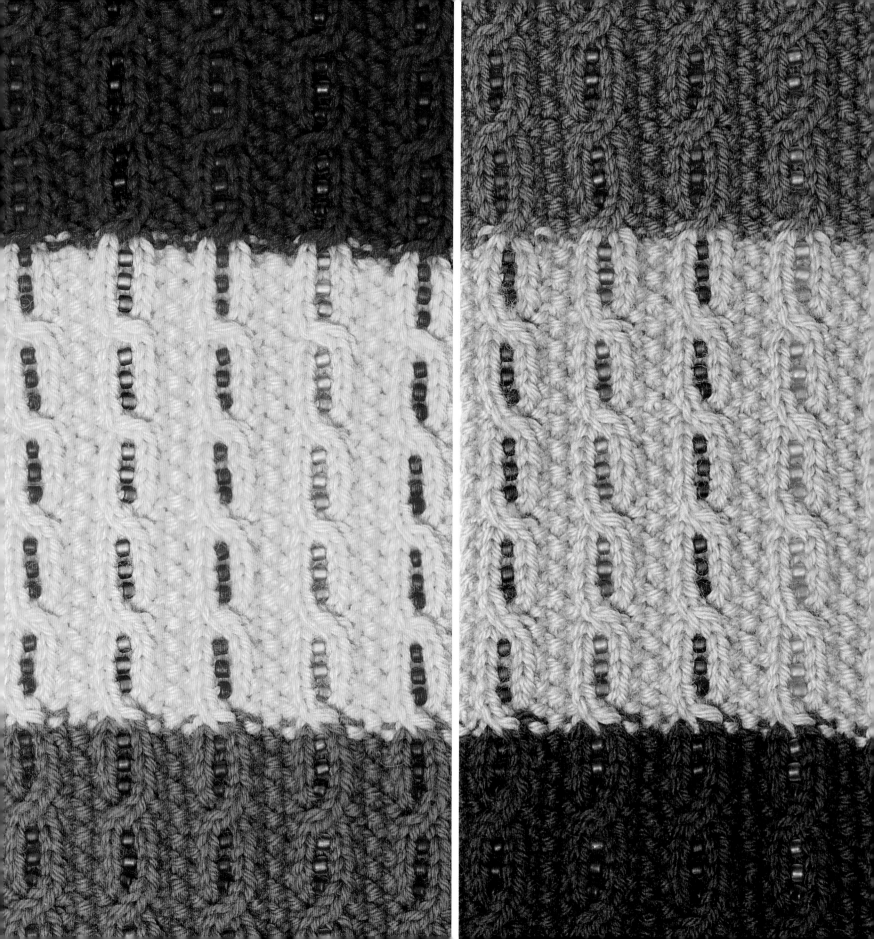

Change to yarn F.
Rep from ** to **.
Change to yarn A.
Rep Rows 47–48 once.
Rep all of the instructions once
more, beg from row 1 of the cable
and bead patt rep and using the
yarns in the same sequence: A
(which you are already using), B, C,
D, E and F, and then the last 2
rows with yarn A again.
Cont to use yarn A only and work
as folls:

Rep rows 1–8, 4 times.
Rep rows 1–5 once.
NEXT ROW (WS): K1, p29, k1.
With RS facing and using yarn A,
cast (bind) off sts knitwise.

FINISHING

Sew in any loose ends on the WS
of the work.

With WS facing and using a
pressing cloth, lightly press the
scarf.

Make 6 small pom-poms: two in
D, one each in B, C, E and F.

Using photograph as a guide,
attach the pom-poms to each
finished short edge as foll: F, C,
and D on one edge and B, E and D
on the other edge.

Electric Satchel

The zany, bright stripes and horizontal bands of beaded zigzags in this design were inspired by musical sound waves. The bag is big enough to carry favourite gadgets and toys, making it the ideal vehicle to transport belongings between school and home or to a friend's house for a sleepover.

SIZE
Approximately 25cm × 22cm (10in × 8½in).

MATERIALS
Pair 3.00mm (US 2–3) needles
Pair 3.75mm (US 5) needles
One circular 3.00mm (US 2–3) needle 60cm (23½in) long

Yarn
Rowan *Handknit Cotton*
50g (1¾oz) per ball
    (A) 315 Double choc   2
    (B) 313 Slick   2
    (C) 324 Bermuda   2

Extras
Beads: 196 × 5mm (³⁄₁₆in) blue beads
2 Buckles: metal alloy, flat-sided, 4.5cm (1.8in) × 2.5cm (1in), opening across is 4cm (1½in)
4 Silver press studs

TENSION (GAUGE)
22 sts and 30 rows to 10cm (4in) measured over stocking (stockinette) stitch using 3.75mm (US 5) needles

KNIT
Base panel
Cast on 55 sts using yarn A and 3.00mm (US 2–3) needles.

Knit 32 rows (garter stitch), ending with a WS row.
With RS facing and using yarn A, cast (bind) off sts loosely and evenly.

Back panel
With RS facing and using 3.00mm (US 2–3) needles and yarn B, pick up and knit 55 sts along cast-on edge of base panel.
*Change to 3.75mm (US 5) needles.
NEXT ROW (WS) (INCREASE): Using yarn B, inc once purlwise into first st, P to last 2 sts, inc once purlwise into next st, p1. (57 sts)
NEXT ROW (RS): Using yarn B, knit.
NEXT ROW (WS): Using yarn C, purl.
NEXT ROW (RS): Using yarn C, knit.
NEXT ROW (WS): Using yarn B, purl.
NEXT ROW (RS): Using yarn B, knit.
NEXT ROW (WS): Using yarn B, purl.

STRIPE PATT REP:
NOTE: Do not break off yarns at the end of rows. Carry them up the side of the work.
ROW 1 (RS): Using yarn A, knit.
ROW 2 (WS): Using yarn A, purl.
ROW 3 (RS): Using yarn A, knit.
ROW 4 (WS): Using yarn C, purl.
ROW 5 (RS): Using yarn C, knit.
ROW 6 (WS): Using yarn A, purl.
ROW 7 (RS): Using yarn A, knit.
ROW 8 (WS): Using yarn A, purl.
ROW 9 (RS): Using yarn B, knit.
ROW 10 (WS): Using yarn B, purl.

ROW 11 (RS): Using yarn B, knit.
ROW 12 (WS): Using yarn C, purl.
ROW 13 (RS): Using yarn C, knit.
ROW 14 (WS): Using yarn B, purl.
ROW 15 (RS): Using yarn B, knit.
ROW 16 (WS): Using yarn B, purl.
Rep the 16 row stripe patt rep twice more.*
Rep Rows 1–8.

Change to 3.00mm (US 2–3) needles.

NEXT ROW (RS) (DECREASE): Using yarn B, K2tog, K53, K2tog. (55 sts)
Leave sts on a holder.

Front panel

With RS facing and using yarn B and 3.00mm (US 2–3) needles , pick up and knit 55 sts along cast-off edge of base panel.
Rep instructions for back panel from * to *.
Leave sts on a holder.

Side panel 1 (using yarn A only)

With RS facing and the back panel to your left and the front panel to your right, and using 3.00mm (US 2–3) needles, pick up and knit 16 sts along short side edge of base panel.
**NEXT ROW (WS) (INCREASE): Inc once knitwise into first st, K to last 2 sts, inc once knitwise into next st, k1. (18 sts)
ROW 1 (RS): Knit.
ROW 2 (WS): Knit.
ROWS 3–10: Rep Rows 1–2, 4 times.
ROW 11 (RS) (DECREASE): K6, sl 1, k1, psso, k2, k2tog, k6. (16 sts)
ROW 12 (WS): Knit.
ROWS 13–34: Rep Rows 1–2, 11 times.
ROW 35 (RS) (DECREASE): K5, sl 1, k1, psso, k2, k2tog, k5. (14 sts)
ROW 36 (WS): Knit.
ROWS 37–58: Rep Rows 1–2, 11 times.
ROW 59 (RS) (DECREASE): K4, sl 1, k1, psso, k2, k2tog, k4. (12 sts)
ROW 60 (WS): Knit.
ROWS 61–82: Rep Rows 1–2, 11 times.
Leave sts on a holder.**
Break yarn.

Side panel 2 (using yarn A only)

With RS facing and using 3.00mm (US 2–3) needles, pick up and knit 16 sts along the other short side edge of base panel.
Rep instructions for side panel 1 from ** to **.
Do not break yarn.
Press the panels.

Slip sts on holders onto spare needles and join side panels to front panel as foll: with RS facing and using yarn A and 3.00mm (US 2–3) needles, knit across 3 sts of side panel 2, then sl 1, k1, psso, k2, k2tog, k2, k2tog (this is the last st of side panel 2 and the first st of front panel), k55 sts across front panel, k2tog (this is the last st of front panel and the first st of side panel 1), k2, sl 1, k1, psso, k2, k2tog, k3. (75 sts)

Knit 10 rows using yarn A (garter stitch), ending with a RS row.
NEXT ROW (WS): Using yarn A, k2tog, k8, cast (bind) off next 55 sts, k8 (including st already on right-hand needle), k2tog.
This leaves 9 sts on each side of the bag for the strap.
Slip both sets of sts for strap onto two separate stitch holders.

Front flap

Thread 196 beads onto yarn A.
Cast on 53 sts using yarn A and 3.75mm (US 5) needles.
Beg with a RS row, work chart Rows 1–68, rep the 8 st patt rep across row 5 times.
Leave sts on a holder.

CHART

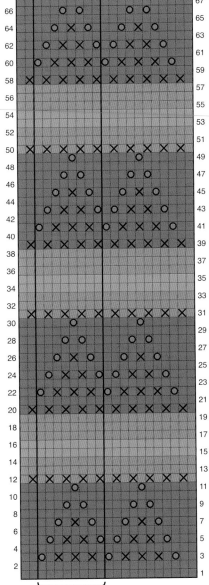

Row numbers on left: 68, 66, 64, 62, 60, 58, 56, 54, 52, 50, 48, 46, 44, 42, 40, 38, 36, 34, 32, 30, 28, 26, 24, 22, 20, 18, 16, 14, 12, 10, 8, 6, 4, 2

Row numbers on right: 67, 65, 63, 61, 59, 57, 55, 53, 51, 49, 47, 45, 43, 41, 39, 37, 35, 33, 31, 29, 27, 25, 23, 21, 19, 17, 15, 13, 11, 9, 7, 5, 3, 1

8 st patt rep

Key
- ▨ A (K on RS)
- ▨ B (K on RS)
- ▨ C (K on RS)
- ⊠ A (P on RS)
- ⊠ C (P on RS)
- ○ Blue bead

Edging (for front flap)

With RS facing and using yarn C and 3.00mm (US 2–3) circular needle, pick up and knit 51 sts down one side edge of front flap, 51 sts along cast-on edge of front flap and 51 sts up the other side edge of front flap. (153 sts)

NEXT ROW (WS): Using yarn C, knit.

NEXT ROW (RS) (INCREASE): Using yarn C, k50, M1, k1, M1, k51 M1, k1, M1, k50. (157 sts)

With WS facing and using yarn C, cast (bind) off sts neatly and evenly (this is a finished edge). Press the flap.

Top edge of flap

Slip sts on holder for front panel onto a spare needle.

With RS facing and using yarn B and 3.00mm (US 2–3) needles, pick up and knit 2 sts along top edge of bermuda garter st edging, knit the first 2 sts of front flap together (these are the first 2 sts on the needle), k49 sts across front flap, knit the last 2 sts of front flap together (these are the last 2 sts on the needle), pick up and knit 2 sts along top edge of bermuda garter stitch edging. (55 sts)

NEXT ROW (WS): Using yarn B, knit. Knit 14 rows using yarn B (garter stitch), ending with a WS row. Do not break yarn.

Join front flap to back panel as folls:

Slip sts on holder for back panel onto a spare needle.

Hold the two sets of sts with RS facing together and, using a third needle, cast (bind) off the sts together.

Lower strap (make both sides the same)

With RS facing, slip 9 sts on holder for strap onto a 3.00mm (US 2–3) needle and, using B, knit 20 rows (garter stitch).

cast (bind) off sts.

Using photograph as a guide, thread strap through lower opening of buckle and sew it down neatly onto the inside of the bag (across the top of side panel).

Strap (make 1)

Using yarn A and 3.00mm (US 2–3) needles, cast on 9 sts.

NEXT ROW (RS): Using yarn A, knit.

NEXT ROW (WS): Using yarn A, k1, p7, k1.

Rep the last 2 rows 7 times more.

STRIPE PATTERN REP:

NOTE: Do not break off yarns at the ends of rows. Carry them neatly up the side of the work.

ROW 1 (RS): Using yarn B, knit.

ROW 2 (WS): Using yarn B, knit.

ROW 3 (RS): Using yarn A, knit.

ROW 4 (WS): Using yarn A, knit.

Rep these 4 rows until the strap is the desired length.

NEXT ROW (RS): Using yarn A, knit.

NEXT ROW (WS): Using yarn A, k1, p7, k1.

Rep the last 2 rows 7 times more.

cast (bind) off sts.

FINISHING

Sew in any loose ends on the WS of the work.

Sew side seams of back and front panels to side panels.

Using photograph as a guide, attach two press studs on the stockinette stitch section at each end of the strap.

Thread each end of the strap through the upper opening of the buckles (one on each side of the bag) and snap the press studs together to close them.

Lining is optional.

Out for the Day

Scrooge Wrist-warmers

Your wrists need never be cold again with these soft warmers knitted in beautiful baby alpaca. They fit right over your knuckles and up to your elbows, leaving your fingers free. They are perfect to wear on a summer's evening when the temperature has cooled down, or they are just as useful on a cold winter's night, when they can be tucked under the sleeves of your sweater and coat to provide an extra layer of insulation.

SIZE
One size

MATERIALS
Pair 4.00mm (US 6) needles
Pair 3.75mm (US 5) needles
Pair 3.25mm (US 3) needles
Cable needle

Yarn
Rowan *Classic Baby Alpaca DK*
50g (1¾oz) per ball
(A) 208 Southdown		1
(B) 204 Zinc		2
(C) 201 Chambray		1

Extras
Beads: 168 × 3mm (⅛in) green
   iridescent beads
28 Small, round, shell buttons

TENSION (GAUGE)
22 sts and 30 rows to 10cm (4in)
measured over stocking
(stockinette) stitch using 4.00mm
(US 6) needles

SPECIAL ABBREVIATION
c3f = (worked on WS rows): slip
next 2 sts onto cable needle and
hold at front of work (this is
towards you, on the WS), p1 from
LH needle then p2 from cable
needle.

c8b = (worked on RS rows): slip
next 5 sts onto cable needle and
hold at back of work, k3 from LH
needle, slip 2 sts back onto LH
needle and knit them, then k3 from
cable needle.

KNIT
Left wrist-warmer
(Begin at the arm and work up to
the wrist.)
*Thread 28 beads on yarns A, B,
and C.
Cast on 72 sts using yarn A and
4.00mm (US 6) needles.
ROW 1 (RS): Using yarn A, p2, (k1,
pb, k1, p2) 14 times.
ROW 2 (WS): Using yarn A, k2, (p3,
k2) 14 times.
ROW 3 (RS): Using yarn A, p2, (k3,
p2) 14 times.
ROWS 4–5: Rep Rows 2–3.
ROW 6 (WS): Using yarn A, k2, (c3f,
k2) 14 times.
ROWS 7–10: Rep Rows 1–4.
ROW 11 (RS): Using yarn B, p2, (k3,
p2) 14 times.
ROW 12 (WS): Using yarn B, k2,
(c3f, k2) 14 times.
ROW 13 (RS): Using yarn B, p2, (k1,
pb, k1, p2) 14 times.
ROW 14 (WS): Using yarn B, k2,
(p3, k2) 14 times.
ROW 15 (RS): As Row 11.
ROW 16 (WS): As Row 14.
ROWS 17–22: Rep Rows 11–16.
ROWS 23–24: Rep Rows 11–12.

ROW 25 (RS): Using yarn C, p2, (k1,
pb, k1, p2) 14 times.
ROW 26 (WS): Using yarn C, k2,
(p3, k2) 14 times.
ROW 27 (RS): Using yarn C, p2, (k3,
p2) 14 times.
ROWS 28–31: Rep Rows 26–27
twice.
ROW 32 (WS): As Row 26.
ROW 33 (RS): Using yarn C, p2,
(c8b, p2) 7 times.
ROWS 34–37: Rep Rows 26–27
twice.
Change to 3.75mm (US 5)
needles.
ROW 38 (WS): Using yarn B, k2,
(p3, k2) 14 times.
ROW 39 (RS): Using yarn B, p2, (k3,
p2) 14 times.
ROWS 40–41: Rep Rows 38–39
once.
ROW 42 (WS): As Row 38.
ROW 43 (RS): Using yarn B, p2,
(c8b, p2) 7 times.
ROWS 44–51: Rep Rows 38–39,
4 times.
ROW 52 (WS): Using yarn A, k2,
(p3, k2) 14 times.
ROW 53 (RS): Using yarn A, p2,
(c8b, p2) 7 times.

ROW 54 (WS): As Row 52.
ROW 55 (RS): Using yarn A, p2, (k3,
p2) 14 times.
ROWS 56–61: Rep Rows 52 and
55, 3 times.
ROW 62 (WS): As Row 54.
ROWS 63–64: Rep Rows 53–54.
ROW 65 (RS): Using yarn B, p2,
(k3, p2) 14 times.
ROW 66 (WS): Using yarn B, k2,
(p3, k2) 14 times.
ROWS 67–72: Rep Rows 65–66,
3 times.
ROW 73 (RS): Using yarn B, p2,
(c8b, p2) 7 times.
ROW 74 (WS): Using yarn B, k2,
(p3, k2) 14 times.*
ROW 75 (RS): Using yarn B, p2,
(k3, p2) 4 times, k1, cast (bind) off
next 6 sts, patt to end.
ROW 76 (WS): Using yarn B, k2,
(p3, k2) 8 times, p1, turn work,
cast on 6 sts above bound (cast)
off sts of previous row, turn work
again, patt to end.
**ROW 77 (RS): Using yarn B, (p2,
k3, p2) 14 times.
ROW 78 (WS): As Row 74.
Change to 3.25mm (US 3)
needles.

On solid ground

If grey isn't your colour, why not choose something else that
matches your wardrobe? You don't have to work in stripes
either – they would look great knitted in a solid colour.

ROW 79 (RS): Using yarn C, p2, (k3, p2) 14 times.

ROW 80 (WS): Using yarn C, k2, (p3, k2) 14 times.

ROW 81 (RS): Using yarn B, p2, (k3, p2) 14 times.

ROW 82 (WS): Using yarn B, k2, (c3f, k2) 14 times.

ROW 83 (RS): Using yarn C, p2, (k1, pb, k1, p2) 14 times.

ROW 84 (WS): As Row 80.
With RS facing and using yarn B, cast (bind) off sts in rib.**

Right wrist-warmer

Rep instructions for left wrist-warmer from * to *.

ROW 75 (RS): Using yarn B, p2, (k3, p2) 8 times, k1 cast (bind) off next 6 sts, patt to end.

ROW 76 (WS): Using yarn B, k2, (p3, k2) 4 times, P1, turn work, cast on 6 sts above cast off sts of previous row, turn work again, patt to end.

Rep instructions for left wrist-warmer from ** to **.

FINISHING

Sew in any loose ends on the WS of the work.

Using photograph as a guide, sew buttons to the edge of the wrist-warmers, positioning them just above the cast-on edge.

The panels can be pressed before sewing the palm seams together: a light misting with water is recommended rather than pressing with an iron.

Sew palm seams together.

Rascal Scarf

This vibrantly coloured scarf will brighten up any outfit for a day in town. The handy pockets at each end of the scarf can be used to store things or used to warm up your hands.

SIZE

Approximately 11.5cm (4½in) wide and 180cm (71in) long, including pockets

MATERIALS

Pair 3.25mm (US 3) needles
Pair 3.75mm (US 5) needles
Pair 4.00mm (US 6) needles
Cable needle

Yarn

Rowan Pure Wool DK
50g (1¾oz) per ball ball

(A) 009 Ultra Marine	1
(B) 039 Lavender	2
(C) 040 Tangerine	2
(D) 006 Pier	2

Extras

Beads: 128 × 5mm (³⁄₁₆in) blue
   iridescent beads
2 Shell buttons

TENSION (GAUGE)

28 sts and 36 rows to 10cm (4in) measured over cable and bead pattern using 3.75mm (US 5) needles

KNIT

The scarf is knitted in two sections, which are joined together after knitting.
Rep the instructions for pocket front, pocket back and scarf twice.

Pocket front

Cast on 33 sts using yarn A and 4.00mm (US 6) needles.
Beg with a RS row, work Rows 1–12 from chart.
Rep chart Rows 1–12 once more.
Rep chart Rows 1–2 once.

Change to 3.25mm (US 3) needles.
NEXT ROW (RS): Using yarn D, p1, (k1tbl, p1) 16 times.
NEXT ROW (WS): Using yarn D, k1, (p1tbl, k1) 16 times.
NEXT ROW (RS): Using yarn B, p1, (k1tbl, p1) 7 times, k2tog, yfwd, (k1tbl, p1) 8 times.
NEXT ROW (WS): Using yarn B, k1, (p1tbl, k1) 16 times.
NEXT ROW (RS): Using yarn C, p1, (k1tbl, p1) 16 times.
NEXT ROW (WS): Using yarn C, k1, (p1tbl, k1) 16 times.
NEXT ROW (RS): Using yarn A, p1, (k1tbl, p1) 16 times.
Cast (bind) off sts purlwise using yarn A.

Pocket back

With RS facing and using yarn A and 3.25mm (US 3) needles, pick up and knit 33 sts along the cast-on edge of the pocket front.
NEXT ROW (WS): Using yarn A, knit.
Change to 3.75mm (US 5) needles.
NEXT ROW (RS): Using yarn A, knit.

STRIPE PATTERN REP:
ROW 1 (WS): Using yarn C, purl.

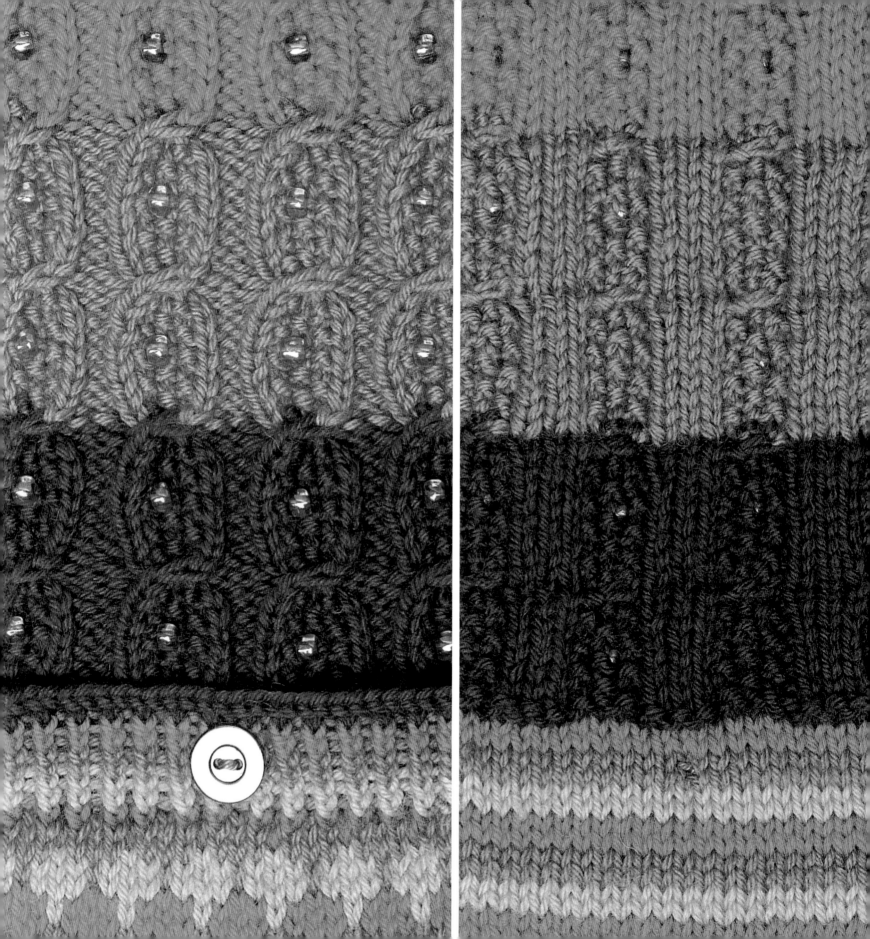

CHART

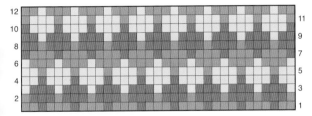

12 10 8 6 4 2

11 9 7 5 3 1

Key

- ▨ B (K on RS)
- ▨ C (K on RS)
- ☐ D (K on RS)

ROW 2 (RS): Using yarn C, knit.
ROW 3 (WS): Using yarn D, purl.
ROW 4 (RS): Using yarn D, knit.
ROW 5 (WS): Using yarn B, purl.
ROW 6 (RS): Using yarn B, knit.
Rep Rows 1–6, 5 times in total.
Rep Rows 1–2 once.

Break off all yarns and thread 16 beads onto each ball of yarn (A, B, C and D).
NEXT ROW (WS): Using yarn A, purl.
NEXT ROW (RS): Using yarn A, purl.

Scarf

NOTE: The right side of the work now becomes the wrong side.
Change to 4.00mm (US 6) needles.
NEXT ROW (RS) (DECREASE): Using yarn A, sl 1, k1, psso, [(k1, p1) twice, k1, p3] 3 times, (k1, p1) twice, k1, k2tog. (31 sts)
NEXT ROW (WS): Using yarn A, p3, k1, p2, (k3, p2, k1, p2) 3 times, p1.
NEXT ROW (RS): Using yarn A, k2, [(p1, k1) twice, p3, k1] 3 times, (p1, k1) twice, k1.
NEXT ROW (WS): Using yarn A, p3, (pb, p2, k3, p2) 3 times, pb, p3.
NEXT ROW (RS): Using yarn A, k2, [(p1, k1) twice, p3, k1] 3 times, (p1, k1) twice, k1.
NEXT ROW (WS): Using yarn A, p3, k1, p2, (k3, p2, k1, p2) 3 times, p1.
NEXT ROW (RS): Using yarn A, k2, [(p1, k1) twice, p3, k1] 3 times, (p1, k1) twice, k1.

NEXT ROW (WS): Using yarn A, p3, k1, p2, (k3, p2, k1, p2) 3 times, p1.

CABLE AND BEAD PATTERN REP:
(Use yarn A for the next 10 rows.)
ROW 1 (RS): K1, (sl next 4 sts onto cable needle and hold at back of work, k1 from LH needle, slip 3 sts back onto LH needle and p1, k1, p1, then k1 from cable needle, p3) 3 times, sl next 4 sts onto cable needle and hold at back of work, k1 from LH needle, slip 3 sts back onto LH needle and p1, k1, p1, then k1 from cable needle, k1.
ROW 2 (WS): P3, k1, p2, (k3, p2, k1, p2) 3 times, p1.
ROW 3 (RS): K2, [(p1, k1) twice, p3, k1] 3 times, (p1, k1) twice, k1.
ROW 4 (WS): P3, k1, p2, (k3, p2, k1, p2) 3 times, p1.
ROW 5 (RS): K2, [(p1, k1) twice, p3, k1] 3 times, (p1, k1) twice, k1.
ROW 6 (WS): P3, (pb, p2, k3, p2) 3 times, pb, p3.
ROWS 7–10: Rep Rows 3–4 twice.

Change to yarn B and rep Rows 1–10 twice.
Change to yarn C and rep Rows 1–10 twice.
Change to yarn D and rep Rows 1–10 twice.
Change to yarn A and rep Rows 1–10 twice.
Change to yarn B and rep Rows 1–10 twice.
Change to yarn C and rep Rows 1–10 twice.
Change to yarn D and rep Rows 1–10 twice.

*Change to yarn A and rep rows 1–10 but omit beads from row 6 as folls:
ROW 6 (RS): P3, k1, p2, (k3, p2, k1, p2) 3 times, p1.*

Rep from * to * using yarn B.
Rep from * to * using yarn C.
Rep from * to * using yarn D.
Rep from * to * using yarn A.
Rep from * to * using yarn B.
Rep from * to * using yarn C.
Rep from * to * using yarn D.
Rep from * to * using yarn A.

Rep from * to * using yarn B.
Rep from * to * using yarn C.
Rep Rows 1–5 using yarn D.
Leave sts on a holder.

FINISHING

Darn in ends carefully on the WS of the work so that they don't show. Block both panels so that the cable and bead section is stretched out to the same width as the Fair Isle/stripe section.

With WS facing and using a damp pressing cloth and a moderate iron, lightly press the panels.

Join side seams of the pockets, making sure that the ribbing at the top edge of the pocket front matches the last stripe on the pocket back. To join the two panels together, slip the sts onto two separate 4.00mm (US 6) needles and using a third needle, cast (bind) off the sts together. Sew buttons on pocket fronts to correspond with buttonholes.

Sweetheart Vest

You really will be noticed out on the streets if you wear this funky, Fair Isle vest! Sparkling pink and purple beads are scattered across this traditional pattern to create an eye-catching garment that will certainly turn heads. It looks great worn over a shirt or T-shirt, or it's just as good worn close to the skin if you feel daring enough!

SIZE

To fit bust

S	M	L	XL	
81–86	91	97	102–107	cm
32–34	36	38	40–42	in

Actual width

43	47	51	54.5	cm
17	18½	20	21½	in

Length to shoulder

53	54.5	60	61	cm
21	21½	23½	24	in

MATERIALS

Pair 3.25mm (US 3) needles
Pair 4.00mm (US 6) needles
One 3.25mm (US 3) circular
  needle, 40cm (16in) long

Yarn

Rowan *Pure Wool DK*
50g (1¾oz) per ball

	S	M	L	XL
(A) 036 Kiss	2	2	2	2
(B) 009 Ultra-marine	2	2	2	2
(C) 039 Lavender	1	1	1	1
(D) 019 Avocado	1	1	1	1
(E) 040 Tangerine	1	1	2	2
(F) 032 Gilt	1	1	1	1
(G) 006 Pier	1	1	1	1

Extras

Beads (4mm/⅛in):

	Purple	(approximate number)	
390	440	490	540

	Pink	(approximate number)	
180	195	210	235

TENSION (GAUGE)

26 sts and 28 rows to 10cm (4in) measured over Fair Isle pattern using 4.00mm (US 6) needles

KNIT

Back panel

*Thread 88 (96: 104: 112) pink beads on yarn D.
Thread 44 (48: 52: 56) purple beads on yarns F and G.
Cast on 114 (122: 134: 142) sts using yarn A and 3.25mm (US 3) needles.
NEXT ROW (RS): K2, (p2, k2) 28 (30: 33: 35) times.
NEXT ROW (WS): P2, (k2, p2) 28 (30: 33: 35) times.
These 2 rows form the rib.
Cont in rib for a further 10 rows, dec 1 st at each end of the last row of small and large sizes only and ending with a WS row.
(112: 122: 132: 142) sts.
Change to 4.00mm (US 6) needles.
NOTE: Omit beads on the first and last sts of rows throughout the panel.
Beg with row 1 of the Fair Isle chart, using the Fair Isle technique and beg and ending rows as indicated for the different sizes, rep the 10 st patt rep across each row 11 times until chart Row 34 completed.
Rep chart Rows 1–34 once more.
L AND XL SIZES ONLY: Rep chart Rows 1–17.
ALL SIZES: Working in stocking (stockinette) stitch (knit on RS rows, purl on WS rows), work 4 (4: 3: 3) rows using yarn B, ending with a WS row.
Beg with row 1 of the bead and stripe chart and beg and ending rows as indicated, rep the 10-st patt rep across each row 11 times until chart Row 14 completed.

SHAPE ARMHOLES

Keeping stripe patt as set by the last 14 rows correct throughout, shape armholes as folls:
NEXT ROW (RS): Cast (bind) off 6 (8: 10: 11) sts at beg of row, work to last 2 sts, k2tog.
NEXT ROW (WS): Cast (bind) off 6 (8: 10: 11) sts at beg of row, work to end.

[(99: 105: 111: 119) sts] *
Dec 1 st at each end of next 5 (7: 9: 11) rows, then on foll 4 (4: 4: 5) alt rows.
[81 (83: 85: 87) sts]
Cont straight until armhole measures 19 (20: 20: 21) cm, ending with a WS row.

SHAPE SHOULDERS AND BACK NECK

Keeping stripe patt correct throughout, cast (bind) off 9 (9: 9: 9) sts, K until there are 13 (13: 13: 14) sts on right needle and turn, leaving rem sts on a holder.

CHART

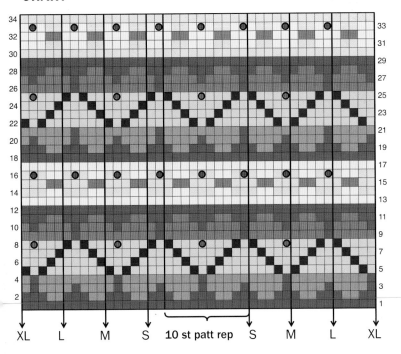

XL · L · M · S · 10 st patt rep · S · M · L · XL

Key

- ■ A (K on RS)
- ▦ B (K on RS)
- ▨ C (K on RS)
- ☐ D (K on RS)
- ▥ E (K on RS)
- ☐ F (K on RS)
- ☐ H (K on RS)
- ◉ Pink bead
- ◉ Purple bead

Work each side of neck separately.
Cast off 4 sts at beg of next row.
Cast off rem 9 (9: 9: 10) sts.
With RS facing, rejoin yarn to rem sts, cast off centre 37 (39: 41: 41) sts, K to end.
Complete to match first side, reversing all shapings.

Front panel

Work as given for back from * to *.
Keeping stripe patt correct throughout, cont as folls:
Dec 1 st at each end of next 5 (7: 9: 11) rows, then on foll 1 alt row. [87 (89: 91: 95) sts]
Work 1 row, ending with a WS row.

SHAPE NECK
Keeping stripe patt correct throughout, shape neck as foll:
NEXT ROW (RS): K2tog, k28 (29: 29: 31) and turn, leaving rem sts on a holder.
NEXT ROW (WS): Cast (bind) off 2 sts at the beg of next row, work to end of row.
Dec 1 st at neck edge on the next 4 (5: 5: 4) rows, then on foll

2 (2: 2: 3) alt rows, then on 1 foll 4th row AND AT THE SAME TIME dec 1 st at armhole edge of next and foll 1 (1: 1: 2) alt rows.
18 (18: 18: 19) sts.
Keeping stripe patt correct throughout, cont straight until front matches back to start of shoulder shaping, ending with a WS row.

SHAPE SHOULDER
Keeping stripe patt correct throughout, cast (bind) off 9 (9: 9: 9) sts at beg of next row.
Work 1 row.
Cast (bind) off rem 9 (9: 9: 10) sts.
With RS facing rejoin yarn to rem sts, cast off centre 27 (27: 29: 29) sts, work to end of row.
Complete to match first side, reversing shapings.

FINISHING

Sew in any loose ends on the WS of the work.
With WS facing and using a pressing cloth, lightly press the panels.

Key

- ■ A (K on RS)
- ▦ B (K on RS)
- ▨ C (K on RS)
- ☐ D (K on RS)
- ▥ E (K on RS)
- ☐ F (K on RS)
- ☐ H (K on RS)
- ◉ Pink bead
- ◉ Purple bead

Join both shoulder seams.
Join side seams on back and front panels

Neckband

With RS facing and using yarn A and 3.25mm (US 3) circular needle, pick up and knit 34 (35: 37: 37) sts down left side of neck, 27 (27: 29: 29) sts from front, 34 (35: 37 37) sts up right side of neck, then 45 (47: 49: 49) sts from back.
[142 (144: 152: 152) sts, or as many sts are required for the sts to sit evenly.]
NOTE: You are now knitting in the round.
Mark the beginning of the round.
ROUND 1: **P2, k2, rep from ** to end.
Rep the last round 6 times more.
Cast (bind) off in rib.

Armhole borders

(Both alike.)
With RS facing and using yarn A and 3.25mm (US 3) circular needle, pick up and knit 92 (100: 112: 116) sts evenly all round armhole edge, or as many sts are required for the sts to sit evenly.
NOTE: You are now knitting in the round.
Mark the beginning of the round.
ROUND 1: **P2, k2, rep from ** to end.
Rep the last round 6 times more.
Cast (bind) off in rib.
Sew in any loose ends on the WS of the work.

CHART

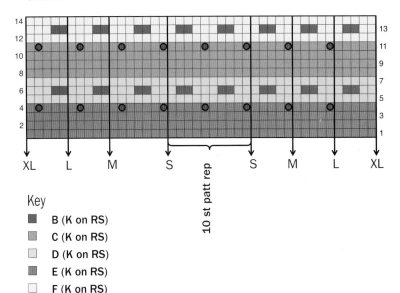

XL · L · M · S · 10 st patt rep · S · M · L · XL

Key

- ▦ B (K on RS)
- ▨ C (K on RS)
- ☐ D (K on RS)
- ▥ E (K on RS)
- ☐ F (K on RS)
- ◉ Purple bead

Book Pouches

This pattern shows how one design can be altered in shape and colourway to give you two pouches for two different purposes. One has a handy ribbon tie to keep everything safely inside it; the other has a button fastening to help keep your books clean and safe.

SIZE

Pouch 1: Approximately 18cm × 14cm (7in × 5½in), excluding flap.
Pouch 2: Approximately 18cm × 23cm (7in × 9in), excluding flap.

MATERIALS

Pair 3.00mm (US 2–3) needles
Pair 2.75mm (US 2) needles

Yarn
(Pouch 1)
Rowan *Cotton Glace*
50g (1¾oz) per ball
  (A) 819 In the pink   2

(Pouch 2)
Rowan *Cotton Glace*
50g (1¾oz) per ball
  (B) 814 Shoot   2

Extras
(Pouch 1)
Beads (3mm/⅛in): 300 pale pink ("pink"), 300 silver ("silver") beads
Beads (5mm/³⁄₁₆in): 25 pale pink ("large pink"), 25 silver ("large silver) beads
Beads (10mm/⅜in): 2 round pink beads
10 Shell buttons (in assorted shapes if preferred)
Ribbon 30cm (12in) long

(Pouch 2)
Beads (3mm/⅛in): 492 blue ("blue"), 432 silver ("silver") beads
Beads (5mm/³⁄₁₆in): 77 red ("large red") beads
3 Large shell buttons

TENSION (GAUGE)

26 sts and 42 rows to 10cm (4in) measured over beaded pattern using 3.00mm (US 2–3) needles

KNIT
Front panel
(Pouch 1)
*Thread beads on yarn A in the foll sequence:
  (5 silver, 1 pink) twice; 5 silver, (2 silver, 2 pink) twice; 2 silver, 3 large pink, (2 silver, 1 pink, 1 large silver, 1 pink) twice; 2 silver, (2 silver, 2 pink) twice; 2 silver, (1 silver, 5 pink) twice; 1 silver, (1 pink, 5 silver) twice; 1 pink, (2 pink, 2 silver) twice; 2 pink, 2 large pink, (1 pink, 1 large silver, 1 pink, 2 silver) twice; 1 pink, 1 large silver, 1 pink, (2 pink, 2 silver) twice; 2 pink (5 pink, 1 silver) twice; 5 pink.

Rep this sequence once more.*

(Pouch 2)
Thread beads on yarn B in the foll sequence:
  (1 blue, 5 silver) twice; 1 blue, (2 blue, 2 silver) twice; 2 blue, 2 large red, (1 blue, 1 large red, 1 blue, 2 silver) twice; 1 blue, 1 large red, 1 blue, (2 blue, 2 silver) twice; 2 blue, (5 blue, 1 silver) twice, 5 blue, 7 blue, 1 large red, 2 blue, 1 large red, 15 blue, **(1 blue, 5 silver) twice; 1 blue, (2 blue, 2 silver) twice; 2 blue, 2 large red, (1 blue, 1 large red, 1 blue, 2 silver) twice; 1 blue, 1 large red, 1 blue. (2 blue, 2 silver) twice; 2 blue, (5 blue, 1 silver) twice; 5 blue, (5 silver, 1 blue) twice; 5 silver, (2 silver, 2 blue) twice; 2 silver, 3 large red, (2 silver, 1 blue, 1 large red, 1 blue) twice; 2 silver (2 silver, 2 blue) twice; 2 silver (1 silver, 5 blue) twice; 1 silver**

Rep the sequence from ** to ** once more.

  (1 blue, 5 silver) twice; 1 blue, (2 blue, 2 silver) twice; 2 blue, 2 large red, (1 blue, 1 large red, 1 blue, 2 silver) twice; 1 blue, 1 large red, 1 blue, (2 blue, 2 silver) twice; 2 blue, (5 blue, 1 silver) twice; 5 blue.

(Both Pouches)
Cast on 49 sts using 3.00mm (US 2–3) needles.
NEXT ROW (RS): Knit.
NEXT ROW (WS): Purl.

(Pouch 1)
Beg with a RS row work Rows 1–24 from chart.
Rep chart Rows 1–24 once more.

(Pouch 2)
Beg with a RS row work chart Rows 1–24.
Rep chart Rows 1–24 once more.
Work chart Rows 1–12 once.
Work chart Rows 25–36 once.
Work chart Rows 1–12 once.

(Both Pouches)
Change to 2.75mm (US 2) needles and cont to work as foll:
NEXT ROW (RS): K1, (p1, k1) 24 times.
NEXT ROW (WS): K1, (p1, k1) 24 times.
Rep the last two rows once more.
Knit 3 rows.
With WS facing cast (bind) off sts knitwise.

Back panel
(Pouch 1)
Rep instructions for back panel from * to *.

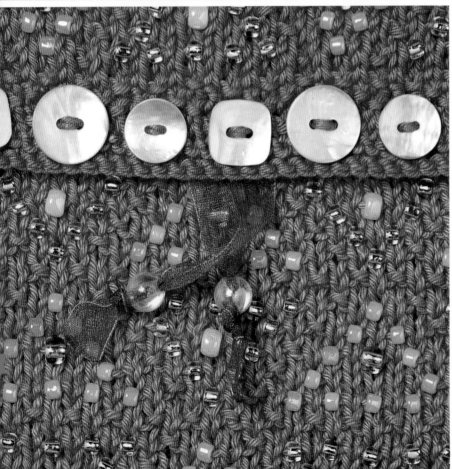

(Pouch 2)
Rep instructions for front panel from ** to **, 3 times in total.
(1 blue, 5 silver) twice; 1 blue (2 blue, 2 silver) twice; 2 blue 2 large red, (1 blue, 1 large red, 1 blue, 2 silver) twice; 1 blue, 1 large red, 1 blue, (2 blue, 2 silver) twice; 2 blue (5 blue, 1 silver) twice; 5 blue.

(Both Pouches)
With RS facing and using 2.75mm (US 2) needles, pick up and knit 49 sts along the cast-on edge of the front panel.
NEXT ROW (WS): Knit.
Change to 3.00mm (US 2–3) needles.
NEXT ROW (RS): Knit.
NEXT ROW (WS): Purl.
Beg with a RS row chart work rows 1–24.
Rep chart Rows 1–24 once more.

(Pouch 2)
Rep chart Rows 1–24 once more.
Rep chart Rows 1–12 once.

(Both Pouches)
Change to 2.75mm (US 2) needles and cont to work as folls:
NEXT ROW (RS): K1, (p1, k1) 24 times.
NEXT ROW (WS): K1, (p1, k1) 24 times.
Rep the last two rows once more.
Knit 4 rows.
Break yarn to thread on beads for flap.

Flap
(Pouch 1)
Rep instructions for front panel from * to *, but DO NOT rep the sequence again.

(Pouch 2)
Rep instructions for front panel from ** to **.
Re-join yarn (A to Pouch 1 and B to Pouch 2), and change to 3.00mm (US 2–3) needles.
NEXT ROW (RS) (DECREASE): K2tog, k45, k2tog. (47 sts)
NEXT ROW (WS): K1, p1, k1, p41, k1, p1, k1.

(Pouch 1)
Beg with a RS row work chart Rows 1–24, cont to work the first and last 3 sts on every row in moss (seed) stitch, as foll:
CHART ROW 1 (RS): K1, p1, k1, work 41 sts from chart, k1, p1, k1.
CHART ROW 2 (WS): K1, p1, k1, work 41 sts from chart, k1, p1, k1.
When chart Rows 1–24 are completed, change to 2.75mm (US 2) needles.
NEXT ROW (RS): K1, (p1, k1) 23 times.
NEXT ROW (WS): K1, (p1, k1) 23 times.
Rep the last two rows once more.
Knit 3 rows.
With WS facing cast (bind) off sts knitwise.

(Pouch 2)
Beg with a RS row chart work Rows 13–24 then chart Rows 1–12 as indicated on the chart for flap, cont to work the first and last 3 sts on every row in moss (seed) stitch, as foll:
CHART ROW 1 (RS): K1, p1, k1, work 41 sts from chart, k1, p1, k1.
CHART ROW 2 (WS): K1, p1, k1, work 41 sts from chart, k1, p1, k1.
When chart Rows 13–24 and 1–12 are completed, change to 2.75mm (US 2) needles.

CHART

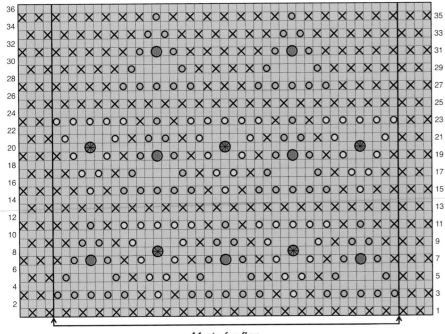

41 sts for flap

Key

▢	B (K on RS)
⊠	B (P on RS)
◯	small bead
○	small bead
●	large bead
✳	large bead

NEXT ROW (RS): K1, (p1, k1)
23 times.
NEXT ROW (WS): K1, (p1, k1)
23 times.
Rep the last two rows once more.
NEXT ROW (RS) (BUTTONHOLE): K6,
(cast (bind) off next 3 sts knitwise,
k13 which includes st already on
right-hand needle) twice, cast
(bind) off next 3 sts, k6 which
includes st already on RH needle.
NEXT ROW (WS): K6, (turn work,
cast on 3 sts, turn work, k13)
twice, turn work, cast on 3 sts, turn
work, k6.
Knit 3 rows.
With WS facing cast (bind) off sts
knitwise.

FINISHING

(Both Pouches)
Sew in any loose ends on the WS
of the work.
    With WS facing and using a
pressing cloth, lightly press the
pouch.
    Sew together the side edges of
the front and back panels.

(Pouch 1)
Using photograph as a guide, sew
the shell buttons onto the edge of
the flap.
Cut the ribbon into two pieces of
equal length. Sew one to the inside
of the case at top edge of back
panel (before beginning of flap),
ensuring that it is in the centre.
Rep for front panel.

Thread one round pink bead onto
each ribbon and knot after the
beads to secure them.

(Pouch 2)
Using photograph as a guide, sew
the shell buttons to the back panel
to correspond with the buttonholes
on the flap.
Lining is optional.
Measure width of finished case
and add on seam allowance.
Measure depth of case, add on
2cm (¾in) for hem allowance and
then multiply by 2.
Cut lining to these measurements.
With RS together fold in half
across width of fabric and sew
together side seams.
Press seams open. Turn to RS.

Turn pouch inside out and slip
lining over pouch with WS together,
matching side seams. Fold a 2cm
(¾in) hem to inside and slip stitch
the lining into place just below the
top edge of the bag and the flap.

Summer Top

Subtle, transparent beading on crisp cotton creates an understated but glamorous design which would look great worn to any summer party. The bright and vibrantly coloured flowers falling around the shoulders and neckline are charming and will make you feel special on any occasion.

SIZE

To fit bust

XS	S	M	L	XL	
81	86	91	97	102	cm
31	33	35	38	40	in

Actual width

40.5	43	45.5	48.5	51	cm
16	17	18	19	20	in

Length to shoulder

58	58.5	59.5	59.5	60.5	cm
23	23	23½	23½	24	in

MATERIALS

Pair 3.25mm (US 3) needles
Pair 3.00mm (US 2–3) needles
Pair 2.75mm (US 2) needles
3.25mm (US 3) crochet hook

Yarn

Rowan *Cotton Glace*
50g (1¾oz) per ball

	XS	S	M	L	XL
(A) 819 In the pink					
	2	2	2	2	2
(B) 814 Shoot					
	1	1	1	1	1
(C) 825 Buttercup					
	1	1	1	1	1
(D) 787 Hyacinth					
	5	5	5	6	6

Extras

Beads (3mm/⅛in):
Purple (approximate amount)

900	950	1000	1050	1100

Round shell buttons,
assorted sizes

14	14	14	14	14

TENSION (GAUGE)

25 sts and 34 rows to 10cm (4in) measured over stocking (stockinette) stitch using 3.25mm (US 3) needles

KNIT
Back panel

*Thread beads on yarn C.
NOTE: When yarn runs out, break yarn at side edge, thread beads onto new ball of yarn, rejoin yarn and continue.
Cast on 103 (109: 115: 123: 129) sts using yarn A and 2.75mm (US 2) needles.
NEXT ROW (RS): K1, (p1, k1) to end of row.
NEXT ROW (WS): K1, (p1, k1) to end of row.
Rep the last 2 rows 13 times more.
Change to 3.00mm (US 2–3) needles.
NEXT ROW (RS): Using yarn B, (k1, p1) 3 times, K to last 6 sts, (p1, k1) 3 times.
NEXT ROW (WS): Using yarn B, (k1,p1) twice, k1, P to last 5 sts, (k1, p1) twice, k1.
Rep the last 2 rows 3 times more.
NEXT ROW (RS): Using yarn C, (k1, p1) 3 times, K to last 6 sts, (p1, k1) 3 times.
NEXT ROW (WS): Using yarn C, (k1,p1) twice, k1, P to last 5 sts, (k1, p1) twice, k1.
Rep the last 2 rows once more.

NEXT ROW (RS): Using yarn C, (k1, p1) 3 times, K to last 6 sts, (p1, k1) 3 times.
NEXT ROW (WS): Using yarn D, k1, P to last st, k1.
NEXT ROW (RS): Using yarn D, k1, (pb, k1) to end of row.
NEXT ROW (WS): Using yarn D, k1, P to last st, k1.
NEXT ROW (RS): Using yarn D, k2, (pb, k1) to last st, k1.
NEXT ROW (WS): Using yarn D, k1, P to last st, k1.
NEXT ROW (RS): Using yarn D, k1, (pb, k1) to end of row.
NEXT ROW (WS): Using yarn D, k1, P to last st, k1.
Place a marker at each end of the last row.
Change to 3.25mm (US 3) needles.
Cont to work using yarn D only.
Beg with a RS row, work 2 rows in stocking (stockinette) stitch (knit on RS rows, purl on WS rows).
NEXT ROW (RS) (DECREASE): K3, ssk, K to last 5 sts, k2tog, k3.
[101 (107: 113: 121: 127) sts]
Purl 1 row.
NOTE: Omit beads on first and last sts of rows.
Beg with row 1 of the beaded chart, and beg and ending rows as indicated on the chart for different sizes, rep the 8 st patt rep across each row 9

times until chart row 28 completed, AND AT THE SAME TIME cont to dec at each side edge as set, on the next row and every foll 4th row until 87 (93: 99: 107: 113) sts rem, ending with a WS row.
Keeping beaded patt correct, work 12 rows in stocking (stockinette) stitch.
Keeping beaded patt correct and taking extra sts into the patt, cont as folls:
NEXT ROW (RS) (INCREASE): K3, M1, K to last 3 sts, M1, k3.
[89 (95: 101: 109: 115) sts]

Work 5 rows in stocking (stockinette) stitch.
Cont to inc at each side edge as set on the next and every foll 6th row until 93 (99: 105: 113: 119) sts, then on every foll 8th row until 101 (107: 113: 121: 127) sts.
Cont to work straight until work measures 38 (39: 39: 40: 40) cm from the cast-on edge.

ARMHOLE SHAPING
(Keep beaded patt on yarn D correct throughout)
Cast (bind) off 4 (4: 5: 6: 7) sts at beg of next 2 rows.
[93 (99: 103: 109: 113) sts]
Dec 1 st at each end of next 5 (7: 7: 9: 9) rows, then on foll 6 (6: 7: 7: 8) alt rows ending with a WS row.
[71 (73: 75: 77: 79) sts]*
Work 3 rows in stocking (stockinette) stitch (knit on RS rows, purl on WS rows).
Beg with row 1 of the chart for yoke, and beg and ending rows as indicated on the chart for different sizes, work until chart row 48 completed, ending with a WS row.

SHAPE SHOULDERS AND BACK NECK
Cast (bind) off 5 sts at beg of next 2 rows. [61 (63: 65: 67: 69) sts]
NEXT ROW (RS): Cast (bind) off 5 (5: 5: 5: 6) sts, knit until there are 9 (9: 10: 10: 10) sts on RH needle and turn, leaving rem sts on a holder.
Work each side of neck separately.
Cast (bind) off 4 sts at beg of next row.
Cast (bind) off rem 5 (5: 6: 6: 6) sts.
With RS facing, rejoin yarn to rem sts and cast off centre 33 (35: 35: 37: 37) sts, knit to end.
Work to match first side, reversing shapings.

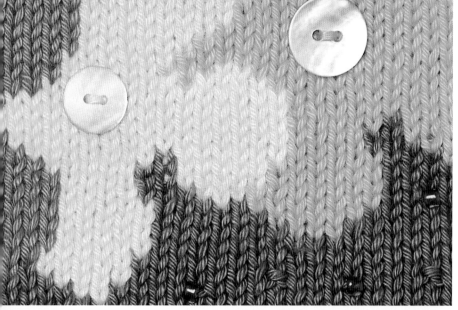

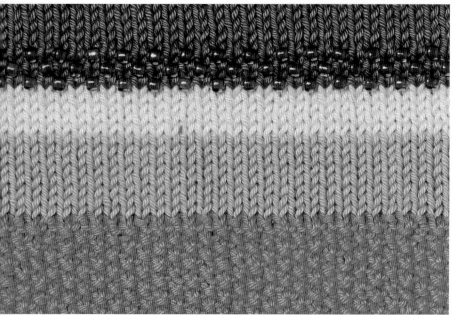

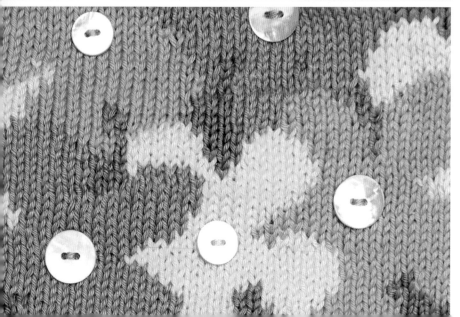

Front panel

Work as given for back from * to *.
Purl 1 row.
Divide for front opening, keep beaded patt on yarn D correct throughout.
NEXT ROW (RS): K35 (36: 37: 38: 39) sts and turn, leaving rem sts on holder.
Work each side separately.
Purl 1 row.
Beg with row 1 of the chart for yoke, and beg and ending rows as indicated on the chart for different sizes, work until 19 (19: 19: 21: 21) rows less have been worked than on back to start of shoulder shaping, ending with a RS row.
SHAPE NECK (cont to work from chart while shaping neck)
NEXT ROW (WS): Cast (bind) off 9 (10: 10: 10: 10) sts at beg of next row and 4 sts at beg of foll alt row.
[22 (22: 23: 24: 25) sts]
Dec 1 st at neck edge on next 3 rows and then on foll 4 (4: 4: 5: 5) alt rows.
15 (15: 16: 16: 17) sts.
Work 5 rows, ending with a WS row.

SHAPE SHOULDER
Cast (bind) off 5 sts at beg of next row and 5 (5: 5: 5: 6) sts at beg of foll alt row.
Work 1 row.
Cast (bind) off rem
5 (5: 6: 6: 6) sts.
With RS facing, rejoin yarn to rem sts, K2tog, K to end.
Work to match first side, reversing shapings.

FINISHING

Sew in any loose ends on the WS of the work. With WS facing and using a pressing cloth, lightly press the panels. Join both shoulder seams.

Front opening edging

With RS facing and using yarn D and 2.75mm (US 2) needles, pick up and knit 17 (17: 17: 18: 18) sts down left side of split, then 17 (17: 17: 18: 18) sts up right side of split. [34 (34: 34: 36: 36) sts, or as many sts are required for the sts to sit evenly.]
With WS facing and using yarn D, cast (bind) off sts.

Neckband

With RS facing and using yarn D and 2.75mm (US 2) needles, and starting and ending at cast-off edge of front opening, pick up and knit 32 (33: 33: 34: 36) up right side of neck, 41 (43: 43: 45: 45) sts from back, and 32 (33: 33: 34: 36) sts down left side of neck.
105 (109: 109: 113: 117) sts, or as many sts are required for the sts to sit evenly.
Using yarn D and 3.25mm (US 3) crochet hook, make a small crochet loop and attach it to the neck edge at left front opening.
Sew button onto neck edge at right front opening to correspond with loop. With WS facing and using yarn D, cast (bind) off sts.

Armhole borders

(Both alike.)
With RS facing and using 2.75mm (US 2) needles and yarn D, pick up and knit 110 (114: 118: 122: 126) sts evenly all round armhole edge, or as many sts are required for the sts to sit evenly.
With WS facing and using yarn D, cast (bind) off sts.
Starting after the markers to leave a vent at each side, join side seams.
Using photograph as a guide, sew buttons on centre of flowers on yoke.

YOKE

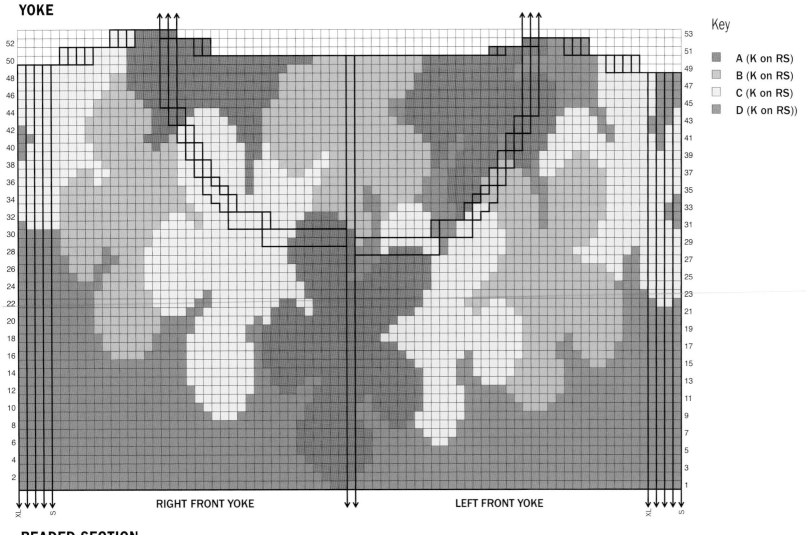

Key

- ▨ A (K on RS)
- ▨ B (K on RS)
- ▨ C (K on RS)
- ▨ D (K on RS))

RIGHT FRONT YOKE

LEFT FRONT YOKE

XL S

XL S

BEADED SECTION

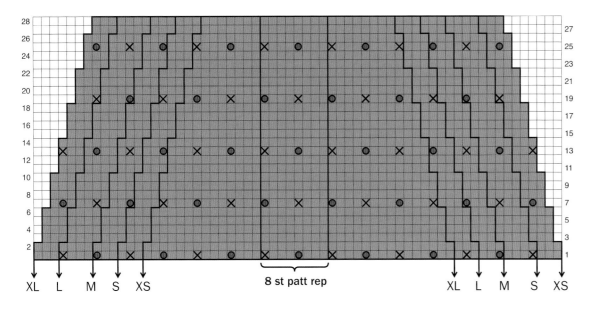

▨ D (K on RS)

✕ D (P on RS)

● Bead

XL   L   M   S   XS

8 st patt rep

XL   L   M   S   XS

Icicle Hat

The beaded cast-on around the edge of this hat creates glistening droplets that look like tiny icicles. The cool, icy theme of this design is strengthened by the use of soft shades of blue in a simple two colour stripe around the hat.

SIZE
One size: approx. 56cm (22in) circumference

MATERIALS
One 4.5mm (US 7) circular needle, 40cm (16in) long
One set 4.5mm (US 7) five dp needles
Cable needle

Yarn
Rowan *Cashsoft Aran*
50g (1¾oz) per ball
  (A) 004 Haze   1
Rowan *Classic Cotton Jeans*
50g (1¾oz) per ball
  (B) 363 Blue wash   1

Extras
Beads: 115 × 5mm (³⁄₁₆in) silver beads

TENSION (GAUGE)
19 sts and 26 rows to 10cm (4in) measured over stocking (stockinette) stitch using 4.5mm (US 7) needles

KNIT
Thread 79 beads on yarn A and 36 beads on yarn B.

Using yarn A and a circular 4.5mm (US 7) needle and thumb method, work beaded cast-on as folls: cast on 3 sts leaving beads at ball side of these sts, *slide bead up yarn so that it is sitting against the needle, cast on another st making sure that the bead is pushed to the RS of the work (facing away from you) as you put the loop onto the needle, cast on 4 sts without beads*, rep from * to * 17 times more, cast on 1 st with bead, cast on 2 sts without beads. (96 sts)

NEXT ROW (RS) (DECREASE) (JOIN THE ROUND): With beads facing toward you and using yarn A, slip the last cast-on stitch (on RH needle) onto the LH needle and knit it together with the first stitch on the LH needle, then knit to end of round. (95 sts)

Mark the first stitch of the round.
ROUND 1: Using yarn A, p2, (k1, p1, k1, p2) 18 times, k1, p1, k1.
ROUND 2: As Round 1.
ROUND 3: Using yarn A, p2, (c3f, p2) 18 times, c3f.
ROUND 4: As Round 1.
ROUND 5 (INCREASE): Using yarn B, K to last st of round, inc once into the last st. (96 sts)
ROUND 6: Using yarn B, k7, (p1, k7) 11 times, p1.
ROUND 7: Using yarn B, knit.
ROUND 8: Using yarn B, p1, (k5, p1, k1, p1) 11 times, k5, p1, k1.
ROUND 9: Using yarn B, knit.
ROUND 10: Using yarn A, k1, (p1, k3, p1, k1, pb, k1) 11 times, p1, k3, p1, k1, pb.

On solid ground

To create a neat beaded cast on, make sure the beads are pushed firmly to the right side of the work before casting on the next stitch.

ROUND 11: Using yarn A, knit.

ROUND 12: Using yarn A, pb, [(k1, p1) twice, k1, pb, k1, pb] 11 times, (k1, p1) twice, k1, pb, k1.

ROUND 13: Using yarn A, knit.

ROUND 14: Using yarn A, k1, (pb, k1, p1, k1, pb, k3) 11 times, pb, k1, p1, k1, pb, k2.

ROUND 15: Using yarn B, knit.

ROUND 16: Using yarn B, k2, (pb, k1, pb, k5) 11 times, pb, k1, pb, k3.

ROUND 17 : Using yarn B, knit.

ROUND 18: Using yarn B, k3, (pb, k7) 11 times, pb, k4.

ROUNDS 19–22: Using yarn A, knit.

ROUNDS 23–26: Using yarn B, knit.

ROUNDS 27–30: Using yarn A, knit.

ROUNDS 31–34: Using yarn B knit.

ROUNDS 35–38: Using yarn A, knit.

SHAPE CROWN (use yarn B only)

NOTE: When there are too few stitches on the needle to continue knitting in the round, split the stitches onto 4.5mm (US 7) dp needles.

ROUND 39 (DECREASE): (K6, k2tog) 12 times. (84 sts)

ROUND 40: Knit.

ROUND 41 (DECREASE): (K5, k2tog) 12 times. (72 sts)

ROUND 42: Knit.

ROUND 43 (DECREASE): (K4, k2tog) 12 times. (60 sts)

ROUND 44: Knit.

ROUND 45 (DECREASE): (K3, k2tog) 12 times. (48 sts)

ROUND 46: Knit.

ROUND 47 (DECREASE): (K2, k2tog) 12 times. (36 sts)

ROUND 48: Knit.

ROUND 49 (DECREASE): (K1, k2tog) 12 times. (24 sts)

ROUND 50: Knit.

ROUND 51 (DECREASE): (K2tog) 12 times. (12 sts)

FINISHING

Run yarn through remaining stitches, draw up and fasten off. Sew in any loose ends on the WS of the work.

Starlight Bag

This casual bag is great for either the town or the beach. Its soft, rounded shape means that you can fit a lot inside it – whether it's your purchases or your beach towel. The denim yarn creates a firm fabric that is very hard-wearing, so if the bag gets dirty or sandy you can stick it in the washing machine and it will come out looking as good as new!

SIZE
Approximately 30cm × 38cm (12in × 15in)

MATERIALS
Pair 3.00mm (US 2–3) needles
Pair 3.25mm (US 3) needles
Pair 4.00mm (US 6) needles
One 3.25mm (US 3) circular needle, 40cm (16in) long

Yarn
Rowan *Denim*
50g (1¾oz) per ball
225 Nashville   6

*This yarn requires a special washing process to finish the fabric. The knitted panels will shrink in length to the correct finished measurements. See instructions at the end of this pattern for how to wash the panels.

Extras
Beads: 166 × 5mm (³⁄₁₆in) blue beads
1 Medium round shell button

TENSION (GAUGE)
22 sts and 28 rows to 10cm (4in) measured over beaded pattern using 4.00mm (US 6) needles

KNIT
Base panel
Cast on 75 sts using 3.25mm (US 3) needles.
Knit 35 rows (garter stitch).
With WS facing, cast (bind) off sts purlwise.

Front panel
Thread 83 beads on yarn.
NOTE: When yarn runs out, break yarn at side edge, thread beads onto new ball of yarn, re-join yarn and continue.
With RS facing and using 3.25mm (US 3) needles, pick up and knit 75 sts along cast-on edge of base panel.
Change to 4.00mm (US 6) needles.
*NEXT ROW (WS) (INCREASE): Inc once knitwise into first st, k4, [(p1, k1) twice, p1, k5] 6 times, (p1, k1) twice, p1, k3, inc once knitwise into next st, K1. (77 sts)
NEXT ROW (RS): K1, [p5, (k1, p1) twice, k1] 7 times, p5, k1.
NEXT ROW (WS): K6, [(p1, k1) twice, p1, k5] 6 times, (p1, k1) twice, p1, k6.
NEXT ROW (RS): K1, p1, [k1, pb, (k1, p1) 4 times] 7 times, k1, pb, k1, p1, k1.
NEXT ROW (WS): K6, [(p1, k1) twice, p1, k5] 6 times, (p1, k1) twice, p1, k6.

NEXT ROW (RS): K1, [p5, (k1, p1) twice, k1] 7 times, p5, k1.
NEXT ROW (WS): K6, [(p1, k1) twice, p1, k5] 6 times, (p1, k1) twice, p1, k6.

BEADED PATTERN REP:
ROW 1 (RS): K2, [(p1, k1) twice, p5, k1] 7 times, p1, k1, p1, k2.
ROW 2 (WS): K1, [(p1, k1) twice, p1, k5] 7 times, (p1, k1) 3 times.
ROWS 3–4: Rep Rows 1–2.

ROW 5 (RS): K2, (p1, k1) 3 times, [pb, (k1, p1) 4 times, k1] 6 times, pb, (k1, p1) 3 times, k2.

ROW 6 (WS): As Row 2.

ROWS 7–8: Rep Rows 1–2.

ROW 9 (RS): K1, [p5, (k1, p1) twice, k1] 7 times, p5, k1.

ROW 10 (WS): K6, [(p1, k1) twice, p1, k5] 6 times, (p1, k1) twice, p1, k6.

ROWS 11–12: Rep Rows 9–10.

ROW 13 (RS): K1, p1, [k1, pb, (k1, p1) 4 times] 7 times, k1, pb, k1, p1, k1.

ROW 14 (WS): As Row 10.

ROWS 15–16: Rep Rows 9–10.

Rep the 16-row patt rep 4 times more, ending with a WS row.
Leave sts on a holder and break yarn.*

Back panel

Thread 83 beads onto yarn.
With RS facing and using 3.25mm (US 3) needles, pick up and knit 75 sts along cast-off edge of base panel.
Change to 4.00mm (US 6) needles.
Rep instructions for front panel from * to *.

Side panel 1

With RS facing and the front panel to your left and the back panel to your right, and using 3.25mm (US 3) needles, pick up and knit 17 sts along short side edge of base panel.

**NEXT ROW (WS) (INCREASE): Inc once purlwise into first st, P to last 2 sts, inc once purlwise into next st, P1. (19 sts)

NEXT ROW (RS): P1, (k1, p1) 9 times.

NEXT ROW (WS): K1, (p1, k1) 9 times.

Rep the last 2 rows twice more, ending with a WS row.

TEXTURED STRIPE PATT REPEAT:

ROW 1 (RS): Purl.

ROW 2 (WS): Knit.

ROWS 3–8: Rep Rows 1–2, 3 times.

ROW 9 (RS): P1, (k1, p1) 9 times.

ROW 10 (WS): K1, (p1, k1) 9 times.

ROWS 11–16: Rep Rows 9–10, 3 times.

Rep the 16 row patt rep, 4 times more, ending with a WS row.
Leave sts on a holder.**
Break yarn.

Side panel 2

With RS facing and using 3.25mm (US 3) needles, pick up and knit 17 sts along the other short (selvedge) edge of base panel.
Rep instructions for side panel 1 from ** to **.
Do not break yarn.
Slip sts on holders onto spare needles and then join side panels to front and back panels as folls: with RS facing and using 3.25mm (US 3) circular needle, knit across 18 sts of side panel 2, sl last st of side panel 2 onto needle holding sts for back panel and knit it together with first st of back panel, knit to last st of back panel, sl last st of back panel onto needle holding sts for side panel 1 and knit it together with first st of side panel 1, knit to last st of side panel 1, sl last st of side panel 1 onto needle holding sts for front panel and knit it together with first st of front panel, knit rem sts of front panel.

NEXT ROW (JOIN THE ROUND): Sl last st of front panel (this is the first st on RH needle), onto LH needle and knit it together with the first st of side panel 2, then purl across all sts. (188 sts)

NOTE: You are now knitting in the round.

Mark the first st of the round.

ROUND 1 (DECREASE): (K2tog, k2) 47 times. (141 sts)

ROUND 2: Purl.

ROUND 3: Knit.

Rep Rounds 2–3, 4 times more.

NEXT ROUND (DECREASE): (K2tog, k1) 47 times. (94 sts)

NEXT ROUND: P9 (these are the sts for first side of strap), cast (bind) off next 10 sts, p18 which includes the st already on RH needle (these are the sts for the tab fastening), cast (bind) off next 10 sts, p9 which includes the st already on RH needle (these are the sts for second side of strap), cast off next 38 sts. Do not break yarn.

Slip the 9 sts for second side of strap and 18 sts onto holders.

NOTE: You are now working back and forth across rows and not on the round.

Strap

Using 3.00mm (US 2–3) needles, cont to work with 9 sts for first side of strap as folls: knit every row (garter stitch) until strap is desired length.

NOTE: The strap will shrink by a small amount after washing, so you will need to knit it slightly longer than the desired length. Leave sts on needle.

To join the strap to the sts for second side of strap (on holder), hold the RS of the strap (without twisting it) against the RS of the bag, slip 9 sts on holder onto a 3.00mm (US 2–3) needle so that the points of both needles are pointing in the same direction, then cast (bind) off the two sets of sts together.

Tab fastening

With RS facing slip 18 sts left on holder onto a 3.00mm (US 2–3) needle and cont as foll:

Knit 16 rows (garter stitch).

NEXT ROW (RS) (BUTTONHOLE): K8, cast (bind) off next 2 sts, K to end.

NEXT ROW (WS): K8, turn work, cast on 2 sts, turn work, K to end.

NEXT ROW (RS) (DECREASE): K2tog, K to last 2 sts, k2tog. (16 sts)

NEXT ROW (WS): Knit.

NEXT ROW (RS) (DECREASE): K2tog, K to last 2 sts, k2tog. (14 sts)

NEXT ROW (WS): Knit.

NEXT ROW (RS) (DECREASE): K2tog, K to last 2 sts, k2tog. (12 sts)

NEXT ROW (WS): Knit.

NEXT ROW (RS) (DECREASE): K2tog, K to last 2 sts, k2tog. (10 sts)

NEXT ROW (WS) (DECREASE): K2tog, K to last 2 sts, k2tog. (8 sts)

NEXT ROW (RS): P2tog, cast (bind) off 5 sts purlwise (1 st rems on LH needle), sl the st on RH needle onto LH needle and purl it together with the rem st on LH needle. Fasten off.

FINISHING

Sew in any loose ends on the WS of the work.

Sew side seams of back and front panels to side panels.

Special washing instructions

Turn the knitted bag inside-out and place it inside a wash bag that can be secured. Wash the bag in a washing machine on the hottest setting so that shrinkage can take place.

Tumble dry the bag until nearly dry. Remove the knitted bag from the wash bag, reshape it and lay it flat to dry.

When the bag is dry, sew button to front panel to correspond with the buttonhole on the tab fastening. Lining is optional.

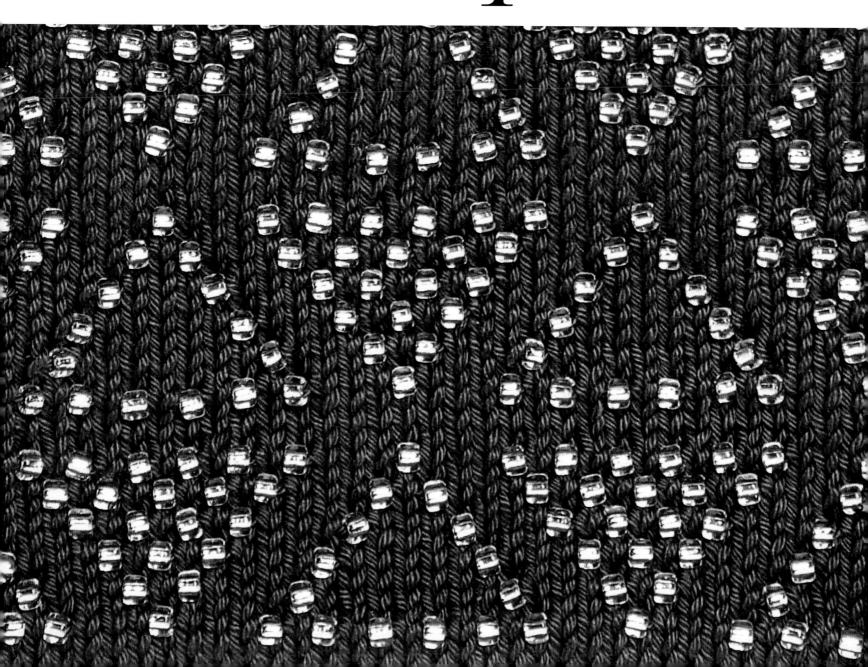

Techniques

KNITTING WITH BEADS

There are many different types of beads available, but not all of them are suitable for hand knitting. When choosing beads it is important to check that the bead hole is big enough for the yarn to pass through. In addition, the weight and size of the beads also needs to be considered. For example, large heavy beads on 4-ply knitting will look clumsy and cause the fabric to sag. It is also wise to check whether the beads you are using are washable, as some may not be.

When you have chosen your beads, you must thread them onto the yarn before you start to knit. There is a very easy way to do this.

Threading beads onto yarn

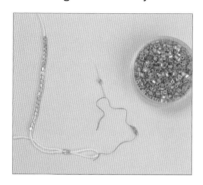

Place a length of sewing cotton beneath the yarn, then bring the two ends of the cotton together and thread both ends through a sewing needle. Thread the beads onto the needle, then push them down the sewing cotton and onto the knitting yarn. Remember that the first bead you thread onto the yarn will be the last one to be knitted in.

ADDING BEADS WITH A SLIP STITCH

This is my preferred method of adding beads to knitting, and it works on both wrong-side and right-side rows. The beads sit in front of a slipped stitch and hang down slightly from where they are knitted in. I have found that if the yarn is held quite firmly and the next stitch after the bead is knitted tightly, the bead sits very neatly and snugly against the knitting.

Adding beads on a right side row

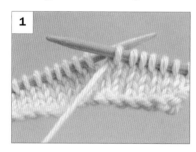

1 Work to where the bead is to be placed. Bring the yarn forward between the points of the needles.

2 Push a bead up the yarn to the front of the work, so that it rests in front of the right-hand needle.

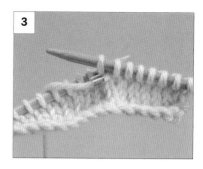

3 Slip the next stitch purlwise from the left-hand to the right-hand needle, leaving the bead in front of the slipped stitch.

4 Take the yarn between the needles to the back of the work and continue in pattern. The bead is now secured in position.

Adding beads on a wrong side row

When beads are placed on a wrong side row, the instructions are almost the same.

1 When a bead is to be added, take the yarn back between the needle points and push a bead up to the front of the work.

2 Slip the next stitch exactly as above.

3 Bring the yarn forward and continue working. On the next row work the slip stitch firmly.

INTARSIA KNITTING

Intarsia knitting produces a single thickness fabric that uses different balls of yarn for different areas of colour. There should be very little, if any, carrying across of yarns at the back of the work.

There are several ways to help keep the separate colours of yarn organized while you are working. My preferred method is to use yarn bobbins. Small amounts of yarn can be wound onto bobbins, which should then be kept close to the back of the work while knitting, and only unwound when more yarn is needed.

The intarsia patterns in this book are given in the form of a chart. It is advisable to make a colour copy of the chart and to enlarge it if you prefer. This copy can be used as a worksheet on which rows can be marked off as they are worked and any notes can be made.

Joining in a new colour

1 Insert the right needle into the next stitch. Place the end of the new pink yarn between the tips of the needles and across the purple yarn from left to right.

2 Take the new pink yarn under the purple yarn and knit the next stitch with it. Carefully move the tail of pink yarn off the right needle as the new stitch is formed.

Changing colours

To avoid gaps between stitches when changing colour, it is essential that the two yarns are crossed over at the back of the work.

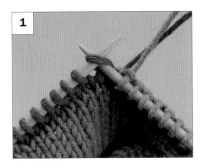

1 On a knit row, insert the right needle into the next stitch. Place the old purple yarn over the new pink yarn. Pull the new pink yarn up and knit the stitch.

2 On a purl row, insert the right needle into the next stitch. Place the old pink yarn over the new purple yarn. Pull the new purple yarn up and purl the next stitch.

Sewing in ends

When an intarsia area is completed, there will be loose ends to darn in on the back of the work.

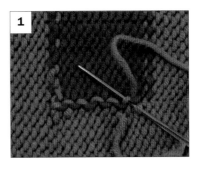
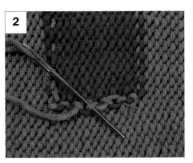

1 Darn the ends around shapes by darning through the loops of the same colour in one direction first.

2 Then darn the end back on itself, stretching the work before cutting the end of the yarn.

KNITTING WITH SEQUINS

Some sequins are plain in colour, but there are also some sequins that resemble mini-holograms, and these create quite spectacular multicoloured effects when held in the light. Sequins not only add extra colour and sparkle to a knitted fabric, but they also change the quality and feel of the knitting.

When choosing sequins, it is important to remember that the hole through the centre must be big enough for the yarn to pass through. The size of the sequin should also be considered, and chosen in relation to the weight of yarn used. And, as with beads, it is also best to check if the sequins are washable before buying them.

The method of adding sequins to knitting is identical to the way that beads are knitted in. However, care should be taken to hold the sequins flat to the fabric while knitting, ensuring that they are all laying the same way. And it is advisable only to place sequins while working on a right side row, as it is extremely difficult to do this on a wrong side row.

ADDING EMBROIDERY TO KNITTING

Outlines, single dots, or fancy shapes and textures can be added to your fabric after knitting. It is advisable to finish your knitting and tidy up the loose ends before embroidering. A large, blunt darning needle should be used to avoid splitting the stitches. A yarn of the same or a slightly heavier weight as the main knitting that will easily cover the stitches is recommended.

I have used Swiss darning in various projects in this book. This is a method of duplicating knitted stitches on stocking (stockinette) stitch fabrics using a needle and a separate length of yarn. It is a quick and easy way of adding dashes of colour or outlines, and it can be worked horizontally or vertically.

FAIR ISLE KNITTING

Stranding is used when the yarn not in use is left at the back of the work until needed. The loops formed by stranding are called 'floats', and it is important to ensure that they are not pulled too tightly when working the next stitch as this will pull in your knitting. If the gap between the colours is more than four stitches, the weaving-in method is preferable as this prevents too long floats that stop the fabric having the right amount of elasticity. Many colour patterns will use both techniques and you will choose the one that is the most appropriate to a particular part of the design.

Stranding

1 On a knit row, hold the first colour in your right hand and the second colour in your left hand. Knit the required number of stitches as usual with the first colour, carrying the second colour loosely across the wrong side of the work.

2 To knit a stitch in the second colour, insert the right-hand needle into the next stitch, then draw a loop through from the yarn held in the left hand – carrying the yarn in the right hand loosely across the wrong side until required.

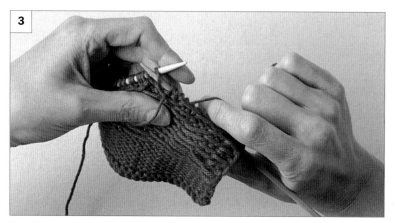

3 On a purl row, hold the yarns as for the knit rows. Purl the required number of stitches as usual with the first colour, carrying the second colour loosely across these stitches on the wrong side of the work.

4 To purl a stitch in the second colour, insert the right-hand needle into the next stitch then draw a loop through from the yarn held in the left hand.

WEAVING

Weaving in, or knitting in, the floats are caught in by the working yarn on every alternate stitch, or preferably on every third or fourth stitch. (Weaving in on every alternate stitch can distort the stitches and alter the tension.) Insert the right-hand needle into the stitch. Lay the contrast yarn over the point of the right-hand needle then knit the stitch in the usual way, taking care not to knit in the contrast yarn. When you knit the next stitch, the contrast yarn will have been caught in. Use the same method to catch in the yarn on the purl rows.

1 On a knit row, hold the first colour in your right hand and the second colour in your left hand. Knit the required number of rows.

CABLES

Cables are the crossing of one set of stitches over another to create a twisted rope effect. Stitches can be crossed over at the front or the back of the work; this determines whether the cable twists to the left or to the right. Stitches held at the front of the work will twist the cable to the left, stitches held at the back of the work will twist the cable to the right. Cables are usually knitted in stocking (stockinette) stitch on a background of reverse stocking (stockinette) stitch, though a background of stocking (stockinette) stitch can also work well. Usually the number of stitches that are crossed are half of the amount stated in the abbreviation, ie: c8b means cross 4 stitches with 4 stitches. There are many different variations, so it is best to read the instructions carefully before starting to knit. This example shows how to work C8B.

C8B

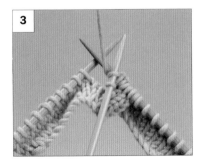

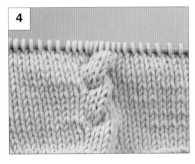

1 Slip the next 4 stitches onto the cable needle and hold at the back of the work.

2 Knit 4 stitches from the left-hand needle.

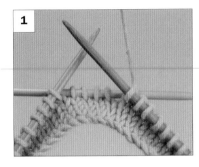

3 Then knit the 4 stitches that are on the cable needle.

4 Make sure that you pull the yarn firmly and knit the stitches tightly to avoid any gaps in the work.

BLOCKING AND PRESSING

The blocking and pressing of knitting is an essential part of the finishing process, and one that is often omitted by knitters. There are several reasons why blocking and pressing should be done. Firstly, it flattens the edges of the knitting, which makes it easier to pick up stitches or sew together panels. Secondly, it ensures that the panels are the correct size. And lastly, it finishes the knitted fabric, and in most cases changes the physical quality of the knitting, smoothing out stitches and making the fabric feel softer and more fluid.

Blocking is the pinning out of the knitted pieces, which should be done on a flat surface with the wrong side facing up. A tape measure should be used to ensure that the pieces are of the correct size. The temperature of the iron used for pressing is dependant on the fibre content of the yarn, as is the damp or dry pressing cloth, which must completely cover the panel that is going to be pressed. The general rule is as follows: natural fibres require a damp pressing cloth and a warm iron, and synthetic fibres and mixes require a dry pressing cloth and a cool iron. However, not all yarns conform to these rules and some have alternative requirements, so it is always advisable to read the pressing instructions that are printed on the ball band. If several different yarns have been used in one piece of knitting, it is better to play safe and follow the instructions for the most delicate yarn. If the heat of the iron is too hot, it could ruin the knitting permanently, resulting in a limp and lifeless piece of knitting that is irreversible.

After pressing it is best to leave the knitting pinned out for at least half an hour to allow all of the heat and moisture to evaporate. Then, when the pins are removed, the knitting will be flat and ready for sewing up.

WASHING AND CARING FOR YOUR KNITTING

Some yarns in this book are machine-washable, however, the item to be washed should be turned inside out and placed inside a protective wash bag to stop the beads from hitting the drum of the washing machine. Always check the ball-band of the yarn for washing instructions before you begin.

Alternatively, you can hand wash your knitting. Use plenty of lukewarm water and a mild detergent specially formulated for knitwear. The fabric should be gently squeezed and then rinsed in several changes of water. It is a good idea to get rid of excess water by placing the knitting in a protective wash bag and gently spinning it in the washing machine. When washing is completed, lay the item on a towel and gently ease it back into shape. It should then be left alone until it is completely dry.

SEWING UP

After spending time knitting, it is very important that the sewing together of the panels is done as neatly as possible. I would recommend that you use mattress stitch, because it is easy to learn, very precise and it creates an almost invisible seam. One big advantage of using this stitch over other methods of sewing up is that you work with the right sides of the knitting facing up towards you, which enables you to see exactly how the seam is progressing. Mattress stitch also allows you to accurately match stripes or patterns on the back and front panels of the bag.

A blunt sewing-up needle and a matching yarn should be used to sew together the panels. Lay the pieces of knitting out on a flat surface in the arrangement in which they are to be sewn together.

Mattress stitch seam (sewing stitches to stitches)

 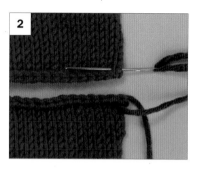  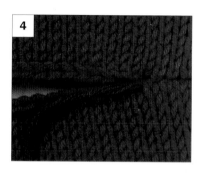

1 From the back of the work, insert the needle through the centre of the first stitch along one of the edges, leaving a long tail of yarn.

2 From the back of the work, insert the needle between the first and the second stitches along the opposite edge.

3 Continue in this way, zigzagging backwards and forwards from edge to edge, and pulling the stitches up to close the seam. Do not pull too hard or the seam will be too tight.

4 The mattress seam is invisible on the right side. Continue sewing the whole seam, then secure the ends by darning them in.

Mattress stitch seam (sewing rows to rows)

 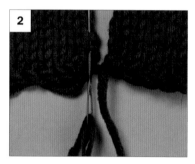  

1 From the front, insert the needle between the first and second stitches on the first row. Take the needle under the next row and bring it through to the front again. Pull the yarn through, leaving a long end.

2 Insert the needle the same way into the other edge that is to be joined, but this time bring the needle out two rows above the point where it goes in.

3 Insert the needle into the first edge again, into the hole that the thread last came out of on that edge. Bring the needle out two rows above that point.

4 Repeat, zigzagging from edge to edge for 5cm (2in). Pull the thread up, holding the seam and long end of the yarn with the left hand.